HIDDEN HISTORY *of* FORT SMITH, ARKANSAS

HIDDEN HISTORY *of* FORT SMITH, ARKANSAS

Ben Boulden

THE History PRESS

Published by The History Press
Charleston, SC 29403
www.historypress.net

First published 2012

ISBN 978.1.60949.450.6

Library of Congress Cataloging-in-Publication Data
Boulden, Ben.
Hidden history of Fort Smith, Arkansas / Ben Boulden.
p. cm.
Includes bibliographical references.
print edition ISBN 978-1-60949-450-6
1. Fort Smith (Ark.)--History. I. Title.
F419.F7B68 2012
976.7'36--dc23
2011052643

Contents

Contents

Preface

One name is on the front of the book identifying me as the author. As in most things, many, many more names and the people who have them were behind the creation of *Hidden History of Fort Smith*.

First, I would like to thank the *Times Record* for allowing me to use the "Inquire Within" columns I have written each week for the newspaper. Although greatly modified and expanded, the writing and information from "Inquire Within" has been the principal foundation for the text of this book. Special thanks go to executive editor Judi Hansen, publisher Gene Kincy and Stephens Media for their openness to the idea.

In corralling the photographs that illustrate this volume, I would especially like to express my gratitude to Caroline Leisa Gramlich and Caroline Speir, both of the Fort Smith Museum of History; Diana Curry of the Fort Smith Public Library; and Janie Glover and Whitney Yoder, both of the Fort Smith Regional Chamber of Commerce.

The core of the photographs here came from the collection of the Fort Smith Museum of History. For more than one hundred years, it has worked to retain and preserve the city's and the region's past. Too often, its importance as a cultural asset has been overlooked and underestimated. I would be greatly remiss if I did the same.

Mark Mondier and Joe Wasson also were great help with photos. Mark is an excellent, skilled, semiprofessional photographer who shot three original photos that are published here. Wasson contributed a rare photo artifact.

Will McKay, an editor at The History Press, first approached me about the possibility of writing a book for them about Fort Smith. He suggested that my columns would be excellent fodder for a "Hidden History" book about Fort Smith. That journey he started for me has led ultimately to the book you now hold in your hand. I thank him for noticing me and "Inquire Within." I also thank him for regarding each as worthy enough to warrant this volume.

I am quite sure I am overlooking someone or someones in all the above credits and statements of gratefulness. I apologize now. Hundreds of readers and local history enthusiasts have contributed information and queries that have only fueled further my deep interest in the stories that surround Fort Smith's past. To them, I also owe much for what is here.

Finally, this book is dedicated to my mother, Katherine Boulden, without whom I would not have any life or become who I am. It equally is dedicated to my wife, Jennifer Marie Boulden, aka The Jenny, without whom that life would not be much worth living.

Introduction

Once upon a time and in my capacity as a reporter, a man asked me if I was going to write the truth in a story for the next day's newspaper. I replied, "I don't write the truth. I write the news." This was greeted with good-natured laughter, but in all seriousness, I explained that only God knows the truth. I can only describe what I have seen and heard people say. I can't peer into someone's heart or soul and with certainty know his or her motives or know the things he is not saying. It is those hidden things that constitute the full truth. In all likelihood, we never will know them in this world. They truly are hidden, as is all history to some degree, if history is truth about the past. What it really is, though, is news of the past—fact-based stories about real events recorded by the people who experienced them or passed down by them through others.

That is not, however, some argument against trying to find the truth. After all, we have our experiences as human beings to draw upon for insight into those unanswerable questions of motivation and meaning. Journalists and historians can attempt to communicate accurately what they and others can observe and experience. Historians in particular can work to tell and discover, retell and rediscover the stories behind the people, places and events of our world.

It is my goal with this book to do that and present the reader with a collection of small historical accounts. Much of what is published in this "Hidden History" are short narratives of the kind that easily might be left out of a traditional narrative history of the city of Fort Smith and its surrounding region. Often we find ourselves spending several minutes looking for some everyday object—car keys, a shoe, a book—that we ultimately find in plain sight or in some location we looked at twice before. If this book makes you say, "Oh, there it is," at least once, then it has done its job.

As part of this book's mission of rescuing the overlooked but interesting from relative obscurity, it also seeks to preserve popular memory of things lost. That's why I have focused on bridges that are gone, creeks buried and people long dead. These things and places once were part of the fabric of everyday life in Fort Smith, sometimes in very significant ways. To understand the generations that came before us here, it's necessary to at least try to comprehend how they lived. By trying to record some of those parts of lost Fort Smith, I hope I have contributed toward that end.

Finally, I could not include everything that ever was in an "Inquire Within" column, nor could I even include everything I wanted to put in it. I am certain there are even more subjects and events that others think should be here. All I can say is that is what other books are for, books that I hope are by me and books by others that are about Fort Smith. Fort Smith has a history rich enough for all of us to mine.

The Fort Cavorts

Wholesome Fun, Playing and Partying

Christmas Beginnings and Traditions

Fort Smith started on Christmas Eve 1817. On that day, the first soldiers arrived by river barge, landed and made camp with the goal of establishing the first fort on the Belle Point bluff overlooking the Arkansas River. Eventually, a village and then a town and finally a city would grow up around it. That first fort was a sort of Christmas gift to the future and the genesis of the city we know today.

As a holiday, Christmas has a special place on the calendar probably without equal throughout the Western world. Much of Fort Smith's celebration of it is not any different than in any other American city. Little about it is at all hidden in history. However, some knowledge about its local celebration has dimmed in memory and is worth remembering again.

A December 1903 edition of the *Fort Smith News Record* recounts how Fort Smith's early settlers marked the holiday. Sophia Barling Kannady was a young Fort Smith woman in the 1840s. She recalled in the story how even the poorest person could feast at Christmas on wild game, ham and turkey. Even large turkeys would go begging for someone to buy them for as little as twenty-five cents.

"People were great on roast pig and a small one in whose mouth an apple would adorn the center of the table," she said. "Then there would be a roast turkey, garnished with parsley, boiled ham, game of all kinds, besides fruits and pastimes. Everything was put on [whole]."

Variously called the Plaza or Town Plaza in the early twentieth century, this is near where downtown Cisterna Park is today on Garrison Avenue between North Tenth and North Eleventh Streets. In the 1920s and 1930s, it was the site for public Christmas celebrations. *Courtesy of the Fort Smith Museum of History.*

According to Kannady, a druggist named "Dr. Meyers" brought the first toys to Fort Smith. He had a shop on Front Street, the main commercial strip in the early city that ran along the river. During the Civil War, parents couldn't get factory-made toys for their children, so adults made them things like dolls from cloth and doughnuts shaped like animals. Kannady said the children appreciated these and enjoyed them just as much.

Many parties took place on the days leading up to Christmas and in the days afterward right up until New Year's Day, but there were none on the day itself, which was treated much like Sunday. No dancing took place on Christmas itself, Kannady said. Candles instead of lamps illuminated the rooms where the parties took place, as did chandeliers with hundreds of multicolored candles on them. Calathumpians, young men in costume and on horseback, would ride through the town whooping and blowing horns.

Also on December 13, 1903, the *Fort Smith News Record* published a feature called "How Weary Willie Spends Christmas: Experiences Related Around the Camp-Fire in the Grove Near the Railroad Crossing." A reporter

Although Christmas lights are hung on Garrison Avenue today, the practice of festooning the thoroughfare with decorations goes back at least to the 1940s. In this image, wreaths and bowers hang in rows over the center of the avenue in the 600 block. The First National Bank building and the Hotel Main are visible to the right. *Courtesy of the Fort Smith Museum of History.*

ventured down to a hobo camp to find out how the transients ordinarily celebrate December 25. One of the camp residents recounted how he and some compatriots had spent the holiday in a cave in a bluff on "the other side of town." His friend Jack went and caught a rooster.

This likely was Bloody Cave, more of a six-foot-deep space underneath a bluff overhang that was used by transients to clean game they had caught. It was that practice that led to its name. One source puts the location of the cave north of Dallas Street in the vicinity of where Fairvew Elementary School is today.

While in New Orleans just before Christmas, a hobo named Joe said he had heard the jail prisoners were going to have a banquet provided for them. He managed to get himself arrested for vagrancy but got sixty days' hard labor and missed the meal.

Another transient said stories of Kentucky hospitality were completely untrue because he had been unable to wheedle a bottle of any spirits out of anyone there. An interesting tidbit gleaned from this 105-year-old story: for cups, the hobos used tin cans with the tops melted off and used a piece of an old cotton bale tie to clean turnips.

A Santa Claus with Saint Bernard dog, circa 1932, stands on the Plaza. Notice the holiday-related displays in the background. This patch of downtown was not always open and was home at different times to businesses such as mule and horse trading. A building for a local jeweler once stood near the spot. *Courtesy of the Fort Smith Museum of History.*

Although hoboes made their own Christmas in Fort Smith more than one hundred years ago, it was provided to prisoners in the U.S. jail at Judge Isaac C. Parker's court. According to the *Fort Smith Elevator* newspaper, they ate a "good Christmas dinner" and listened to music from a chorus of Sunday school children. By 1886, 104 prisoners also consumed turkey, eggnog and cigars; in 1893, there were fruit, cake and onions, besides the usual entrées. A jailer then even made them "a good strong toddy" to drink.

As Fort Smith progressed into the twentieth century, old traditions faded away and new ones came to the fore. Even as early as 1903, Kannady commented that Christmas in Fort Smith had changed. The Plaza on the north side of Garrison Avenue between North Tenth and North Eleventh Streets was the scene of public Christmas celebrations in the 1920s and 1930s. At first, only a lightly decorated tree marked the holiday there, but as time went by, the celebrations added a living Santa, igloos and even fake snow. Because Garrison, not Front Street, had long since become the commercial center of the city where most folks did their Christmas shopping, it seemed only natural to put Santa and the city tree there.

An Arena and a Stadium

Jimmy Lott and his wife, Stella, retired in the early 1970s and moved to Florida. One thing they were unable to pack and take with them—the memories of many people who went to Jimmy Lott's Wrestling Arena to see boxing great Joe Louis referee or Gorgeous George grapple with a foe.

Jimmy Lott first organized bouts at the National Guard Armory on North B Street in the 1950s. Dennis McCaslin, in a telephone interview, said his parents operated the concessions at Lott's, and he even sold Cokes and peanuts, too.

Lott was a former junior heavyweight wrestler who competed in the 1930s and 1940s and then became the local promoter in a wrestling circuit that took in Little Rock, Tulsa, Oklahoma City and Fort Smith. McCaslin confirmed that Gorgeous George did wrestle there in the very early 1960s, along with many other notables. The venue itself had a capacity of about nine hundred.

McCaslin remembered how a wrestling bear got loose from the station wagon his owner drove him around in and ran down Towson Avenue to a café. He said Fort Smith police helped capture him and get him back to Lott's.

Joe, a local kid, remembered how in the 1960s his dad used to take him to watch wrestling matches at Jimmy Lott's. One of his favorite wrestlers was a star-spangled, all-American type who was going up against a villainous foreigner.

Joe, who still was in grade school at the time, was determined to help his hero, so he spent all afternoon sharpening a popsicle stick into a weapon, a sort of shiv. When the bad guy had his good guy pinned to the mat, he stabbed the villain in the bottom of his foot by reaching through the ropes of the ring with the shiv. His victim started howling in pain and limping around the ring. Needless to say, Joe and his dad were tossed out of Jimmy Lott's.

The names of the wrestlers who appeared at Jimmy Lott's were even more colorful than comic book superheroes—Skandor Akbar, Silento Rodriguez and Sputnik Monroe. Many folks recall Skandor and another popular wrestler with a less showy moniker—Danny Hodge. All those guys wrestled at Lott's. Wrestling today has some things in common with wrestling then, but it seems to be a bigger business now without the goofy, relatively more innocent charm of yesteryear.

Before Jimmy Lott's was even an idea, Fort Smithians found athletic entertainment at Stadium Park just a few blocks west of Towson Avenue at South Ninth Street and Carnall Avenue. It was there on May 11, 1916, that then-mayor Henry C. Read led a dedication ceremony opening the park and ball field. Also there on that day, he unveiled for the first time a flag for the city of Fort Smith. Governor-elect C.H. Brough also attended the event, which was preceded by a parade and included flag drill by schoolchildren. The Fort Smith Twins baseball team played another team from Denison, Texas.

To get the new baseball park ready for the ceremony and game, several hundred people showed up a week earlier to celebrate "Board Day," the baseball equivalent of a barn raising. Men and women pitched in to fence it. Carpenters who had been working to build the stands donated a half day of labor to the cause. Everyone worked together to complete the fencing, the *Fort Smith Times Record* reported at the time.

Little is remembered about Stadium Park, and the record remains unclear about exactly what happened to it. Likely, it was supplanted by the creation and opening of Andrews Field a few blocks west of it. Named for John Andrews, who led the campaign for its creation, that field opened for play in May 1921. Stadium Park appears to have been located on a lot that once was home to the first Belle Point School. Today, a wing of the Sebastian County Detention Center sits on it.

THE WATER IS FINE

Swimming was another wholesome activity enjoyed by young people and others. It also was an excellent way of coping with the heat in the first half of the twentieth century in a time before air conditioning. Few public pools existed though. Most were in private hands and charged admission to swimmers. Darby Junior High School, originally Fort Smith High School, did have an indoor swimming pool, and it was one of those public ones back in the day. Often it was left open for use by nonstudents.

Near Midland Boulevard and Kelley Highway, Whittaker Pool in the 1930s and 1940s was a privately owned swimming pool then enjoyed by children of the city. They paid a small admission fee to use it in the warm-weather months. *Courtesy of the Fort Smith Museum of History.*

The Whittaker pool was at 2420 North Thirty-first Street near Kelley Highway and not far from Midland Boulevard and Division Street. According to an old city directory, Robert Poteet owned it between 1942 and 1945. A 1948 directory lists Herbert Henrici as proprietor of the nearby Whittaker Apartments.

Besides the Darby pool and the Wheeler Boys' Club pool, Richard Griffin, who grew up in Fort Smith during those years, said there really wasn't much else that a kid could get access to in the swimming season. He couldn't remember what the fee was to get into the Whittaker pool, but he said it was something "minimal."

In the middle of the pool was a big, metal top. Griffin said it was as big as a small car, shaped like a child's spinning top and probably anchored to the bottom of the pool, although he couldn't swear to that last bit. Kids could climb on it and sit. It would tilt and turn just like a top. Children would try to knock one another off it into the water. Essentially, it appears to have been a safe way to play king of the hill.

According to one correspondent, the giant floating top in the middle of the water was attached to the pool's bottom by a "a curve of spiral steel about one inch in diameter." Although the pool lasted into the early 1960s, sadly, it's gone now, home to a church parking lot.

In regard to privately owned swimming pools to which the public could purchase admission, there also was the Joseph Hurley pool at 1818 South Sixteenth Street, circa 1925. *Southwest Times Record* columnist Tom Blake reported in 1981 that Hurley dug it out by hand, mule and wheelbarrow, and it had a fifty-foot diving platform. In a collection of reminiscences called "Flashbacks," Harry Huey writes that the Hurley pool was "north of the old standpipe and settling basins."

Huey also makes reference to a swimming pool near North Tenth and North A Streets. This may have been more of a swimming hole if it indeed was the same one that is referred to in some early accounts of Fort Smith history. On the northwest corner of North Tenth Street and Garrison Avenue was the Old Red Mill, a planing mill for lumber. It was gone by the first years of the 1900s, but nearby was the small swimming hole that boys used to play in. Floodwaters from Town Branch may have dug it out of the ground and filled it with water. It was extraordinarily deep by most accounts. However, the water often was stagnant and polluted, and adults of the town tried to discourage boys from playing in it.

The Joies of Movie Palaces

No monarchs or emperors ever made their homes in Fort Smith. That doesn't mean Fort Smith was free of palaces of a different sort. Its stately pleasure domes provided interior space for movies to shine forth and allowed audiences to daydream in the dark.

The New Theatre, built circa 1911 at North Tenth Street and Garrison, probably is one of the least hidden and best remembered, in part because it continued to operate until the late 1970s. Over its original main entrance on North Tenth and on the keystone of arched entryway is a gargoyle face and the name "Sparks." Many people mistakenly think that it was first home to Sparks Hospital. It was not.

After his death in a shipwreck off the coast of California, the George T. Sparks Trust funded construction of the theater to provide income for his family. Sparks was one of the first directors of First National Bank of Fort Smith. His family also made a large donation to the Fort Smith hospital and

Across the street from the New Theatre and around the corner from the Joie, the Mystic (center) had its heyday from about 1925 through the 1930s. Later, as Camp Chaffee grew during World War II, the Malco movie company reopened the theatre as the Plaza Theatre. Always a sort of low-rent, second-run theater, the Plaza closed circa 1971 for public health reasons. By all accounts, the Plaza was not a movie palace but fed off diverted traffic from them. *Courtesy of the Fort Smith Regional Chamber of Commerce.*

medical center that still bears their name. It was renamed "Sparks" to honor the gift.

The doors of the New Theatre first opened to general audiences in late September 1911. Its opening bill was *The Third Degree*, a play in four acts by Charles Klein. Live theater and vaudeville acts were its core business in the beginning.

The Sunday, August 13, 1922 edition of the *Southwest American* heralded the opening of what it called fashion's promenade. "Fort Smith enters the truly cosmopolitan class for every large city has its 'Peacock Alley' or its 'Petticoat Lane.'" It was the former name that stuck. Peacock Alley was a grand, two-story shopping arcade with tiled walls, inlaid tile floors and a rounded-arch ceiling over its central passage. Several small shops lined Peacock Alley, which terminated on its north end farthest from Garrison at a second main entrance into the lobby of the New. Under liberal guidelines, it could be called Fort Smith's first indoor shopping mall.

In January 1929, Enid, Oklahoma–based Publix Theatres, which was operating the New Theatre and the Joie (discussed later) by that time, announced both were being wired for Vitaphone and Movietone sound equipment. Talkies had come to Fort Smith. The project cost a total of $20,000. "With the opening of the New Theatre as a Vitaphone house, Fort Smith will be the only city of its size in the southwest with two houses featuring 'talking pictures,'" the *American* stated.

Unlike the New Theatre, few people, if any, have a living memory of the Sebastian Theatre that opened circa 1914 and closed several years later. That's too bad, because enough of its interior features are intact at 615 Garrison Avenue to give a visitor the idea that it must have been wonderful. The Sebastian's interior is graced with Art Nouveau features, including some abstract depictions of female figures in the top corners of the ceiling on the building's second floor.

When theatergoers walked into the Sebastian's auditorium, the ceiling reached all the way up to those cornered females. There was no second floor. Another thing that was different was that upon entry, the screen was to their side and the projector straight ahead near the farthest wall. Audience members had to turn around toward the entrance to see the screen as they took their seats.

Much later, in the postwar heyday of Hollywood and just before the great early expansion of television media, the Rex opened in the 1600 block of Midland Boulevard. Although the building still stands, it has been adapted for use as a cold storage warehouse. The Rex didn't start its life as an entertainment venue as the Rex, however. Edward Lichty and his brothers Ernest and Selwyn launched it in 1946 as the Pix with the plan of showing movies to an exclusively black audience. Attendance wasn't robust enough to sustain it.

Jerry Carson worked at the Rex from 1951 to 1953. He said the Lichty brothers changed the name to the Rex because they only had to pay to switch out two letters. Once the name changed, they opened it to a mixed-race audience but one that still was segregated.

Carson said blacks had a separate side entrance and ticket booth and then climbed to a separate balcony where they could sit. Connie Lichty-Smith remembers a glassed-in crying room also built into the balcony of the Rex. That was where her family often watched movies. Admission in the early 1950s was ten cents.

The Rex was a second-run theater and always showed Westerns for Saturday matinees that were filled with children. Buddy Blair remembers seeing movies there, including the original version of *The Thing That Came from Outer Space*. His parents would drop him off at 1 p.m. on Saturdays. Between the two features, cartoons and serials, he was kept busy until almost 5:30 p.m.

A theater that is completely gone today is Hoyt's Theatre at 12 North Seventh Street. Operation of it may have started sometime between 1920 and 1925 as the Victory Theatre. Hoyt Kirkpatrick took it over around that time and renamed it Hoyt's Theatre. According to a few old-timers and some movie advertisements, Hoyt's tended to show musicals, comedies and family fare like Shirley Temple movies.

A Kentucky native who already was managing theaters in Texas, Kirkpatrick came to Fort Smith in 1912 to assist his recently widowed sister in running the Joie, then located on Garrison Avenue. Kirkpatrick kept expanding and improving the theater there until he ran out of room. In October 1921, he solved that problem by moving the Joie to a sparkling new venue on South Ninth Street between Garrison and Rogers Avenues.

In addition to motion picture shows, like the New Theatre, the Joie offered first-class space to vaudeville acts. Its acts were on the Orpheum circuit. Not all the wonders of the Joie were on stage. The *Southwest American* newspaper at the time describes the lobby and auditorium as having elaborate, decorative woodwork. The lobby floor was covered with a "rich gray carpet from Eads Brothers furniture store" and the lobby walls with mirrors. When viewing a movie or live performance, theatergoers could plant themselves in a seat "padded and upholstered in soft, brown leather." A $4,500 ventilation system kept the air fresh inside.

Other amenities included a cloakroom with an attendant for patrons to check their coats, bags and other outwear and accessories. The Joie even had a playroom called "Baby Land" for children and a former schoolteacher employed there to watch over them. Mothers were encouraged to leave their young children in the playroom so they could enjoy the theater's entertainment without the distraction of childcare.

"Danger of fire is practically eliminated in the fireproof building," the *American* reported in 1921. Sadly, this would prove inaccurate. In December 1953, the Joie was gutted by fire. A few years later, crews demolished what was left of it.

Between the movie palace and the multiplex, between the World War II and the Gulf War and between the parking lot and the indoors, America devised an entirely unique way to enjoy cinema—the drive-in theater. Fort Smith had at least three such notable venues: the Sky-Vue Drive-In Theatre at 5500 Midland Boulevard; the 22 Drive In Theater on the southeast corner of Rogers Avenue and South Seventy-fourth Street; and the 71 near Jenny Lind Road and Zero Street. Although not the movie palaces of old, the drive-ins did offer almost palatial expanses of open space.

J. Fred Brown built the Sky-Vue and opened it in 1961. It closed circa 1985. At the time of its construction, it may have been the largest drive-in movie theater in Arkansas, weighing in at eight acres and six hundred parking spaces. Car-side speakers piped sound into each car. A fully equipped playground featuring an electric merry-go-round was located below and in front of the screen for small children to enjoy.

Violet Burton Isaacks and her husband, Carl, owned and operated the 22 from about 1948 to 1976. Isaacks said she operated it by herself for a few months after Carl's death and then sold the equipment to a Texas theater chain. The 22 occupied about ten acres and had both car-side and outside speakers. For the first ten years it was in business, it exhibited films during all twelve months of the year and then seasonally during much of the 1960s and finally year-round again in the decade before it closed.

Like the Sky-Vue, it, too, had a playground. Its carousel was not electric. For a time, it used sixteen live burros. A go-cart track provided a loop for the racing of those small, fast vehicles there when movies weren't showing.

All three of Fort Smith's drive-ins were gone by the 1980s. They no longer could compete effectively with multiplexes and the videotape rental businesses that allowed families to watch movies at home.

Centers of Attention: The Hotel Main and Goldman Hotel

Together, two Garrison Avenue hotels were the social centers of the city for almost a century. Dr. J.H.T. Main built the 125-room Hotel Main in the early 1880s in the avenue's 600 block. On February 1, 1910, the 175-room Goldman Hotel opened for business at the east end of the avenue in the 1200 block. Both would host weddings, social receptions, meetings and conferences for decades.

According to *Physicians and Medicine* by Amelia Martin, John Hanson Thomas Main was the first civilian physician to settle in Fort Smith. He came here in the 1830s to attend to the men who were building the second Fort Smith, the military fort. An alderman on the first city council, Main also amassed considerable property, including several houses, eleven farms

The Hotel Main, built in the 1880s, was a great social center until the completion of the Goldman in 1910. Behind its ornate Victorian front, it provided lodging to visitors, meeting space to locals and a dining hall and saloon. *Courtesy of the Fort Smith Regional Chamber of Commerce.*

totaling about three thousand acres and the Hotel Main. The hotel had been open less than a decade when Main died on September 3, 1891.

In historic photos of Garrison, the Main, with its ornate late Victorian façade, always seems to stand out if it is anywhere within sight of the camera. All sorts of gatherings took place in the hotel, from official meetings to unofficial ones in smoke-filled rooms. A traveling businessman wanting to make connections and be seen stayed at the Main. There was plenty of room. The layout of the building stretched a block deep from the Garrison front to the Rogers Avenue rear.

A richly appointed dining hall offered some of the best food in the city during the hotel's heyday. Perhaps a good example of what the bill of fare was like is the special holiday menu on Thanksgiving Day 1909. The *Fort Smith Times Record* reported then that it included appetizers of caviar, mangoes and green sea turtle, among other culinary delights; dinner entrées of lobster Newberg, Lake Superior whitefish with lemon butter sauce, suckling pig, roast turkey and southern-style possum; and desserts of hot mince pie, English plum pudding, coconut and almond macaroons, figs, dates, nuts, tutti fruiti ice cream and a huge variety of cheeses. An orchestra provided music for ballroom dancing at the holiday feast, too.

The Goldman Hotel, which opened a little more than two months after the Thanksgiving feast, was no stranger to musical balls, dances and even radio broadcasts. Before it could provide a home for such festivities, the hotel first had to undergo the longer-than-expected struggle to be built. Construction started in 1907 on what was originally planned to be called the Sebastian. Spooked by a market panic, hotel stockholders halted the project with only two stories of the structure complete. According to *A Corner of the Tapestry: A History of the Jewish Experience in Arkansas 1820s–1990s*, one of the investors, Rudolph Ney, contacted a St. Louis cotton magnate and banker, Jacob Goldman, and persuaded him to provide the remaining funds necessary to finish the building. Work on it resumed in April 1908. Despite the St. Louis connection, the Fort Smith Hotel Co., composed of Fort Smith businessmen, was the owner, the *Fort Smith Times Record* reported in 1910. They included Ney, Harry E. Kelley, T.W.M. Boone, James Brizzolara and Wharton Carnall.

From 1910 until well after World War II, the Goldman Hotel was in many ways the social center of the city. It was home to everything from trade shows and conventions to weddings and banquets. A third wing later was added to the north side of the building. *Courtesy of the Fort Smith Museum of History.*

Once finished, six stories of steel-reinforced concrete were arranged into two wings that fronted North Thirteenth Street. The owners advertised the hotel as "fireproof" and "European." A third wing was added in 1919 at the north end to bring the room total to 225. Although the second-floor mezzanine contained suites for offices and showrooms, the basement, first and second floors were public spaces. Hotel rooms composed the third through fifth floors and a large ballroom the sixth.

The Goldman was a classic hotel of bellmen, doormen and other service personnel. Its owners maintained a full staff of 125 to 150 people at its height. Tuxedo-clad waiters served meals with silverware, presented finger bowls and delivered the checks on silver trays. Most local people who ate there maintained accounts at the hotel from which they could even draw cash. A four-chair barbershop could provide a daily shave, as well as a shoeshine, haircut or manicure, to the visiting businessman.

It was the site of visits from the famous as well as meetings of the everyday Rotarian. Among the celebrities who stayed in the Goldman were humorist Will Rogers; film stars Rosalind Russell and Susan Hayward; baseball greats Dizzy Dean and Mickey Mantle; female golf star Babe Dedricksen; and the eight-foot, 11.1-inch tallest man in the world, Robert Wadlow. The Goldman took it in turns with Little Rock and Hot Springs hotels to host state conventions of fraternal and professional organizations. Wholesale businesses and factories often set up sample rooms in the hotel for the examination of area buyers. In 1930, John England, the manger of the Goldman by that time, started what would become the oldest continually operating radio station in Fort Smith, KFPW.

World War II brought contractors working to build and expand Fort Chaffee, as well as military guests. After World War II, the hotel slowly went into decline with the increasing popularity of motels. Commercial air travel also changed the lodging practices of Americans, shifting them away from downtown hotels in cities that were clustered around or near railway stations. Hotel rooms gradually became low-rent apartments instead. In 1974, the city fire marshal closed down the building, declaring it unsafe. An attempt in the late 1980s at restoration failed, and in 1994, Immaculate Conception Church purchased and demolished the property.

The Goldman had long since supplanted the Main when the latter fell on hard times with the Great Depression. Despite new owners and rebranding as the Milner Hotel, it also ultimately closed and fell to the wrecking ball circa 1950. Both places downtown where each hotel once stood are now parking lots.

Rambling Boys of Pleasure and Ladies of Easy Leisure

Prostitution Outside the Row

The Row, a vice district proscribed by city ordinance in 1907, was notorious in its day and still is remembered for its houses of prostitution. It was an area of a few square blocks north of Garrison and very near and parallel to the Arkansas River. From 1907 to 1924, prostitution was legal there and, in the city of Fort Smith, there only. Although it became illegal again even there after repeal of the ordinance, prostitution continued to be tolerated by local law enforcement for decades afterward.

During the legal period, Row prostitutes applied for licenses, paid a monthly license fee and were inspected by the city health inspector twice a month. Madams, or keepers of houses of prostitution, paid a higher license fee monthly. Once it was illegal, fines were levied in the same amounts for prostitutes and madams.

By the time of World War II, there may only have been two houses left operating in the Row—Miss Laura's and Miss Ella's. Bertha Dean, who had been the madam at Miss Laura's on First Street since 1910, died in 1948, marking the end of an era. Ella Scott died in the 1950s, and her house was demolished by the 1960s. Miss Laura's, now the Fort Smith Visitor Center, remains as the sole survivor of the Row and a reminder of that period.

Prostitution activity moved from the Row after Bertha Dean's death into legitimate downtown hotels where men could obtain the services of call girls. It also moved into smaller hotels where prostitutes lived that were little more than bordellos. These latter hotels were in buildings along streets just north of Garrison Avenue.

Buildings don't leave diaries, letters or memoirs. Few prostitutes do either. Prostitution and buildings share something else in that respect. In *Chinatown*, Roman Polanski's 1974 film masterpiece starring Jack Nicholson, the character Noah Cross says, "Respected? Of course, I'm respected. I'm old. Prostitutes, politicians and ugly buildings all become respectable if they last long enough."

It's hard to say if the house that once stood on one of those downtown side streets at 215 North Fourth Street was ugly, but it didn't last forever. It was a rooming house for transients and others. In 1993, Atlas Roofing purchased the land the residential house once occupied, but it was already gone by then.

According to county land records and a city directory, the previous owner and resident was a woman named Vida Reho, who died on April 30, 1991, at age ninety-one. Her obituary lists no survivors. However, the obituary also reports that Reho was the former owner and operator of the Ozark Hotel, which once stood at 122 North Fifth Street.

The Ozark, like the Como Hotel across the street and one block south on Fifth Street, was associated with prostitution. Whether Reho had any direct connection with that business is difficult to say. At least one source states she just rented cheap rooms to people down on their luck at a rooming house at 123 North Fourth and at the Ozark.

Three American Social Health Association (ASHA) reports from the 1960s pretty clearly establish that prostitution activity occurred during that decade at the Ozark. Whether Reho owned the hotel then isn't clear. Nevertheless, Reho's joint ownership of the property at the three addresses plus the Ozark's reputation may have rubbed off on her and her house at 215. No one seems to recall any great tragedy or crime that occurred at the property on 215 North Fourth Street. However, the association reports do provide some interesting details about prostitution activity at the Como, the Ozark and other such Fort Smith "hotels."

"The 'houses' are supposed to be hotels," a 1962 ASHA report quotes one source saying. "They're nothing but real joints." Porters and desk clerks in them served as pimps or procurers for guests seeking the services of a prostitute. Prices ranged from ten dollars to as much as forty-five dollars depending on what was requested.

Three girls in 1962 were working at the St. Charles Hotel at 9 North Fifth Street. The desk clerk there told the association investigator, posing as a customer, that he had nothing to worry about "from the law." One young woman there said she had been working as a prostitute since she was sixteen and had been in the business for nine years.

"Do you want to know why I do this?" she asked. "I do it for one thing and one thing only—money. I like money and all I can get of it."

By the middle of the next decade, the Fort Smith police effectively and permanently would close the Como. The St. Charles and the Ozark would see the same fate and eventually fall to the wrecking ball.

Games of Chance

Fort Smith's reputation in the late 1800s and early 1900s as a wide-open town was not built solely on prostitution in its notorious Row, the city's abundance of saloons or even the outlaws brought in for trial in Judge Parker's court. It also earned some of that reputation from gambling.

According to "The Weaver Papers," soldiers, early settlers and visitors from the countryside frequently gathered to bet on horses at Back Stretch Row, a strip of open flat land that ran several hundred yards north–south from the northwest corner of what is today the intersection of Greenwood and Rogers Avenues. These were straightaway races, unlike ones that made the oval loop around Spring Park.

Spring Park was the horse-racing track that once was located where Ramsey Junior High School is today. Finding information about Spring Park isn't easy, but *Reflections of Fort Smith* by Julia Etter Yadon, Sue Ross Cross and Randall Rose Viguet does have two photos of it and a few paragraphs. Some local historians assert that the site was used for racing horses in the antebellum period. Primary sources confirm other facts that *Reflections* reports.

By circa 1912, Spring Park had a grandstand, ticket office, stables, a restaurant and food stands. The Arkansas-Oklahoma Interstate Fair used the site in 1914 and probably for a few years afterward, too. Some even have suggested that's where Fairview Elementary School nearby got its name. It is next door with a "view" of the old fairgrounds.

Barney Oldfield, the early auto racer, broke his own half-mile speed record there circa 1914. *Reflections* does not record when Spring Park fell into disuse.

Likely, it was a gradual process in which the site eventually was supplanted by Andrews Field and Kay Rodgers Park.

According to the *Fort Smith Times Record*, Harry E. Kelley supervised the extension of the South Twenty-first Street trolley line out to Spring Park to take people to and from the fair. It passed about a block from Kelley's home at South Twenty-second and South W Streets.

Several *Fort Smith News Record* reports in the early twentieth century shed light on gambling activity taking place then in the city. In a 1903 story, an unnamed man of leisure recounts his routine of visiting an establishment called the Turf Exchange, "where the races are taken." A telegraph operator there each day read aloud minute-by-minute accounts of races taking place at that time in cities as distant as New Orleans.

"Racing across the house tops and descending to the street by the scuttle of a building several doors away, a score of men escaped from the room over the Turf billiard hall and so avoided arrest in a personally conducted [raid] by Chief of Police George Moss last night," the *Times Record* reported on April 28, 1912. It's unclear whether the downtown Turf establishment is the same as the one in the 1903 account, but apparently both were homes to gambling. Police seized six craps tables, cards, chips and other paraphernalia, which were taken to a location on Parker Avenue and burned.

Some raids were even more cinematic. Fort Smith police in November 1912 again raided the rooms above the Turf billiard hall. Before the raid, officers watched the gambling going on there through a roof skylight. Once they were convinced they had watched long enough, they smashed in the glass of the skylight with their pistols and then descended into the room on ladders. Officers again seized decks of cards, tables and poker chips, along with a "wagon load of paraphernalia" that was burned at the jail, the *Times Record* reported. The raid was one of several that were conducted in November 1912. In one six-week period in the fall of that year, the police arrested sixty men for gambling. On November 25, 1912, the *Times Record* reported that the crackdown seemed to be having the desired effect. Gamblers were leaving town: "Most of the gamblers went into eastern Oklahoma where it is said plenty of [gambling places] are still found and the police seldom make raids.

The Turf was not the only venue for gambling then. Moss named others in a December 1912 report to a grand jury. Besides the Turf, he included in his list the Stag pool hall and the Star pool hall. Moss stated all the establishments used lookouts and panic buttons with buzzers to try to avoid detection by law enforcement authorities or cops on their beats. He recommended to the grand jury that the licenses of all the pool halls be revoked. With the revocations, the police then could turn their full attention to other gambling dens. "Such places as the Main Hotel, the Southern Hotel and like places where gaming is indulged will receive our attention in such a way that we believe that we will be able to put a full stop to the same," Moss stated.

Police Chief Moss might have done well to mention another hotel, the then-two-year-old Goldman. In April 1913, Earl Frates, eighteen, brought suit against the manager of the hotel to recover $778 he had lost there in a "gentleman's game" of poker. Regular poker games had been conducted at the hotel for several months, the *Times Record* reported. A few days later, several young men from prominent families came before a police court judge and pleaded guilty to criminal charges of gaming with a minor. (At that time, an individual achieved legal status as an adult at twenty-one years of age.) Moss said he arrested the young men to make an example of them and considered the matter closed after that.

His example did not entirely take. By late 1914, the *Times Record* was editorializing against the use of what it called push and pull boards to entice the city's young people into gambling. The newspaper does not describe exactly how these worked, but from what it does describe, they may have been punchboards. A patented and manufactured version of a lottery game board, thirty million punchboards flooded the United States between 1910 and 1915. To win a prize, a punchboard player simply had to pay a penny or a nickel for the privilege of pushing a nail or rod through a small punchboard hole. If the player was successful in pushing out a piece of paper inside the slot and that paper had a number on it corresponding to a prize, then he or she won. "There can be no question that the boards are a detriment to the morals of the young, and to them perhaps may be traced the evidence that gambling in a more pronounced form is again seeking to gain a foothold in the city," the newspaper's editorial page opined.

None of the 1914 stories names the Goldman Hotel as a venue for punchboards. Cigar and newsstands frequently were home to them, and the Goldman's was no exception. Cigar stand girls there reportedly ran a bookmaking operation where their customers could roll dice, "double or nothing," for their purchases. These local women were great sources of local gossip and information.

Gambling today is concentrated in Choctaw and Cherokee casinos just over the border in eastern Oklahoma. State lotteries also offer opportunities to individuals who want to play the odds. Internet sites present similar offerings to players. It now is a big business, leaving little room for pool-hall sharpies like those once found at the Turf.

Wet, Dry, Wet

Nationwide Prohibition in the 1920s and early 1930s successfully destroyed the rich saloon culture of the United States. It destroyed it in Fort Smith, too.

Fort Smith has long enjoyed a reputation for drinking liquor and for liquor establishments. Just a cursory examination of city directories for the years 1894, 1904 and 1911 reveals some startling numbers. In 1894, about 20 saloons had Garrison Avenue addresses; 1904—31; and 1911—42. If saloons and bars just off Garrison on side streets are added in, then those totals move even higher, albeit in single digits. Towson Avenue even had quite a few rough taverns in the nineteenth century, according to "The Weaver Papers." These might have been crude cabins or cribs with a plank bar and a limited menu of drinks. Beer was not unknown in antebellum Fort Smith—the Knobel Brewery was founded in 1848, and in the *Fort Smith New Era* in the late 1870s, a famous Fort Smithian by the name of Valentine Dell heralded in his newspaper the arrival of kegs of beer coming in by train. He expressed the hope that its availability would cause some to abandon whiskey.

Prohibition locally and statewide arrived in 1916, before the Eighteenth Amendment's ratification three years later. The signs of a crackdown on drinking and saloons started to show at least as early as 1912. New local rules initiated in January 1913 forced them to close at 11:00 p.m. In 1910, a new licensing restriction had put closings at midnight. Also, blacks and whites no longer could patronize the same place, even with separate bars inside. Bootleggers, moonshiners and illegal bars likely kept some folks drinking nevertheless. One prominent businessman is reported to have bought all the cases of liquor he possibly could stuff in his basement.

With the end of national Prohibition in 1933, the sale and consumption of beer, wine and liquor became legal again in Arkansas. Some towns and counties stayed dry, exercising local options. A glance at some city directories from the 1930s and 1940s shows that saloons and bars did not immediately return to downtown Fort Smith in great numbers. Liquor stores seem to have been even more common. The saloon's dominance of drinking culture was gone. Perhaps a lingering stigma caused local folks who wanted to drink to discreetly buy a bottle and take it home to imbibe. It seems as though drinking establishments were pushed to the fringes of the city beyond its limits.

South Seventy-fourth Street was called Wildcat Mountain Road before it became part of the city. Although it may at one time have had the name Chaffee Terrace, at least two sources record the Rockwood Club or Rockwood Supper Club near where Horan Drive now intersects South Seventy-fourth Street. It was in a rock house built in the 1920s. By one account, it burned down circa 1953. Another source remembers a Chaffee Terrace on the west side of the street. Neither it nor the Rockwood Club was housed in buildings built by Monsignor Tom Horan, aka Father Horan. However, the Riverview Steak House did occupy a house he owned in the vicinity of where Green Ridge Drive is in east Fort Smith. That establishment reportedly burned in about 1963. (Horan owned much of the land in that part of what is now east Fort Smith.)

Undoubtedly, these places beyond the eastern fringe of the city attracted soldiers from Camp Chaffee seeking a drink and a meal closer to the army base.

Drinking establishments eventually did return to Fort Smith and its downtown. The Branding Iron at 4001 Midland Boulevard opened its doors for drinkers, diners and dancers circa 1953. It remains the oldest bar in the city, although the big bands that played there have long since packed up and left.

Country singer Toby Keith even has immortalized one or two of these post-Prohibition taverns in song. In 2005, his song *Honkytonk U* recounted his time spent with his late grandmother in Fort Smith in a nightclub she owned called Billie's Supper Club. In actual fact, it was Billie Garner's Supper Club at 1521 Rogers Avenue. According to Keith's uncle, a Fort Smith resident, she never owned or ran a place called "Clancy's Tavern"—an album the Nashville artist released in 2011. However, her nickname in the family was Clancy. He said no one outside the family ever referred to her by that name. So the Clancy's Tavern referred to in the album title is really more of a generic.

Clancy, which is what we will call her for our purposes here, worked at Dixie Cup for several years and kept second jobs running a place called Guy's Tavern at 4009 Midland Boulevard and another called the Glass Hat at 522 North Tenth Street. Her husband died at an early age, leaving her with three children to raise on her own. When she had a chance to buy Billie Garner's, Clancy jumped at it. She owned and operated that business for several years until about the time the property sold. Garner had retained ownership of the property.

A GYPSY OASIS

Desert caravans in the Middle East or along the famous Silk Road in Asia stopped at ponds or springs of water in order to rest, water and feed their pack animals. These oases were essential to their survival as they traveled through harsh, dry climates. Although Fort Smith was not in the middle of a desert, it did offer a similar attraction to gypsies traveling through mid-America in the late nineteenth and early twentieth centuries.

Gypsies, more formally known as Roma today, are believed to have originated in northern India and were cast out of their native land. Hundreds of years ago, they began wandering in bands through Europe, northern Africa and the United States. Gypsies never stayed in any one place for very long and earned the unfortunate reputation, probably undeserved, for thieving, kidnapping and deception.

Fort Smith likely did not have a particular geographic or cultural draw for gypsies, but two people who lived here did. William H. and Mary "Marie" L. Cole set up a drugstore at 602 Garrison Avenue in the early 1890s. In May 1891, they both applied to the State of Arkansas to practice pharmacy. Mary Cole thus became the first female licensed pharmacist in the state. According to a neighbor of the Coles, both William and Mary told her the following story separately and at different times.

As newlyweds on their way to Fort Smith, the Coles came upon a large group of gypsies who were in a panic near a river or stream. The Coles learned a girl from the group had fallen into the water and was drowning. William Cole dove into the water and rescued her. From that moment on, the gypsies befriended and admired the Coles. When a band of them was passing through the area, they often would stop to pay their respects to the couple.

Sometime around 1912, Steve Costello, a leader of a Spanish band of gypsies, suggested that Marie Cole become their postmistress. She at first served as postmistress to the Spanish gypsies, but the community she served soon broadened to include other groups. For about the next twenty years, Marie Cole forwarded thousands of letters, along with telegrams and cablegrams.

"Only she knew where to find the persons to whom they were addressed," Edwin Hicks wrote in December 1932. "She made Fort Smith the capital of the gypsy world."

To pay her for her services, gypsies brought her curios, antiques and all sorts of oddities, many of which the Coles displayed in their drugstore. "The

Cole drug store became a veritable museum, a showplace that was visited by persons who came through the city," Hicks wrote. "Visitors inquired where the store was and paid it a call soon after arriving in town. Many were the notables who came there."

In 1910, Fort Smith police arrested about twenty-five to thirty gypsies who had camped out at McNally's Hill, a ridge near today's intersection of Rogers Avenue and Cliff Drive. Some had come there from points in Oklahoma, others from as far away as Chicago.

"There appears to be a movement on foot to assemble a mammoth colony here and engage in the usual business of the Gypsy tribe, that of horse trading, fortune telling etc.," the *Fort Smith Times Record* reported.

For more than a day, the newspaper stated, gypsy men, women and children had been drinking. They also were reported to have been stealing animal feed from nearby farms and generally frightening residents of the area with their loud, raucous behavior.

In August 1911, the *Fort Smith Times Record* reported that gypsies were camped at what is today the intersection of Waldron Road and Rogers Avenue. "They expect to spend several months in this city and vicinity, and it would not be surprising if they took an active interest in the horse features of the coming interstate fair, for the true Gypsies are the most expert horsemen and horse breeders in the world, and they have some fine stock with them," the newspaper states.

The *Times Record* goes on to state that several of the young gypsy women not only were educated but were graduates of Vassar University, and that an exchange of visits was expected between the Coles and the band.

Two disputes between gypsies spilled over into local courts in 1912. According to the *Times Record*, both stemmed from conflicts over marriages between families, unpaid dowries and allegations of money taken. The newspaper, in both cases, describes the young women involved as unusually attractive and "comely."

"A feature of her picturesque dress was that her coal black hair hung in braids over her shoulder and at the end of each there was attached an Austrian ducat gold piece, which is worth about $11 in American coin," a report states. "She was also wearing the now locally famous gold coin necklace, composed of $20 gold pieces."

In January 1914, Steve Costello was a party to another matrimonial dispute between gypsy families. He came to rescue his sister, Columbus, from an abusive husband, George Mendis. Mendis claimed he had paid the Costellos $3,000 in a dowry to marry the young woman. Mendis attempted to get local police to intercede to keep the Costellos from leaving town with his wife. Mendis and a colony of gypsies were camped out near Cliff Drive just east of Fort Smith. He alleged Costello was selling his daughters, taking them back and then reselling them. Police allowed Steve Costello to leave with Columbus.

During an April 1915 visit to the city, a gypsy woman, Lida Young, was arrested for the alleged theft of $225 in cash and a diamond ring from Mrs. James Dobbins. Young had visited the Dobbins home on one or two occasions to tell fortunes.

A so-called "gypsy king," Yanko Urich, died in Fort Smith on February 1, 1923, while his tribe was camped out near Forest Park Cemetery. Urich died of heart failure while undergoing an operation for appendicitis. For a time, his body laid in state in a large tent at the camp. A funeral mass was held for him at Immaculate Conception Church, and then his body and casket were transported in a hearse to the cemetery while the gypsies walked alongside. Funeral dirges also were played as the procession traveled down Midland Boulevard. Once at the cemetery, the gypsies built a bonfire for warmth.

In August 1932, Marie Cole suffered an accident, falling down some stairs at 111 Garrison Avenue. (The Coles had by that time moved their drugstore to that location and moved their home to an apartment on the second floor above.) More than a week later, she died from her injuries while a patient at Sparks Hospital.

Nearing the age of eighty, in May 1934 William Cole was struck by a car while crossing Garrison. He died two days later.

Camping in the same places, gypsies continued to come to the Fort Smith area. Sometime around or just after World War II, however, the frequency of their visits declined and the strength of their presence faded. Within a decade after the death of the Coles, Fort Smith's role as a gypsy oasis came to an end.

Lost and Fading

Places Long Gone or Going

Swastika on the Avenue

Swastikas are peculiar things. On the southwest corner of Garrison Avenue and Ninth Street, at 822 Garrison, there is a two-story building. Its front once was covered with yellow paint and red swastikas—some pointing right and some left. The yellow and red have faded with time, and the symbols are now hard to see but still discernible with a close look.

For many years, a sign that read "Historic Indian Swastika—Original Painting" filled a window space on the building and tried to explain to passersby that it was not a Nazi swastika. At the center of the sign was a swastika symbol, and at its four points were the words "Good Luck—Love—Life—Light."

The words "Inquire Within" were at the bottom of the sign, which was placed there by a previous owner and occupant, Hub Pawn Shop. Hub felt compelled to put up the sign to explain the red swastikas painted all over the yellow background of the building's Garrison front. Those swastikas were revealed after some veneer was removed many years ago during restoration work. The use of the swastika on this building probably had little to do with American Indians, as some have claimed.

A photographic image in *Garrison Avenue: Memories and Photographs* by Stan Kujawa shows the building sometime between 1928 and 1930, when it was occupied by Pollock Chain Stores. Furthermore, it shows the business name on the edge of an awning, along with swastikas. Why a Jewish merchant family like the Pollocks would use swastikas is an even more interesting question that is hard to answer. However, Hitler's rise to power in Germany wasn't really complete

Built in the first decade of the twentieth century, this building (left in block) at 822 Garrison Avenue once was adorned with swastikas visible on its front. Covered over for decades, renovations to the façade in the 1980s revealed them again, and they have faded in the years since. *Photo by Mark Mondier.*

To the left in this picture postcard, 822 Garrison appears to be swastika-free. Originally an ancient symbol for good luck, the Nazis appropriated it as their own. The Jewish owners understandably covered it up as the symbol's meaning changed. *Courtesy of the Fort Smith Museum of History.*

until 1933, probably well after the painting on the store façade was done and before the swastika was so absolutely identified with that evil regime.

A swastika on the exterior of 822 Garrison is fading fast but discernible in this detail shot. *Photo by Mark Mondier.*

Before Hitler's use of it, the swastika was a common, cross-cultural symbol found in American Indian, Hindu, European and other motifs. A swastika pattern appears more subtly in a pressed-tin ceiling in another building on the avenue. City directory ads for Sparks Hospital in the 1920s also use the swastika as a design flourish.

It's possible that the Pollocks borrowed it from an American Indian source or even were trying to use it to appeal to them as buyers, but no direct American Indian connection to the building has been found. Neither directory listings for the address nor Kujawa's book indicates an American Indian presence at 822 Garrison between 1928 and 1930.

Based on other photographs, the swastika design painted on the stonework does not seem to date to its original construction. That paint layer is fading fast, returning the façade to what apparently was its first state—plain, cut stone or block.

The Color Line: Fort Smith in Black and White

Unlike some towns and cities of the Delta region of Arkansas, slave plantations and large populations of African American slaves never surrounded Fort Smith and never had a large presence in western Arkansas.

Based on census records, most slave owners here operating small farms or businesses only held small numbers of slaves. Free African Americans did migrate to the region and city, forming small but significant communities.

Some of these communities were not large enough to support separate public schools, so those cities and towns of western Arkansas later in the twentieth century sent young African American students into Fort Smith to be educated. Public schools for blacks only, like Howard, Washington and Lincoln, provided education through the high school level in the years after the Civil War and until desegregation in the 1960s. Lincoln High School closed in 1966, as its African American students were integrated into the larger white student populations at Northside and Southside High Schools.

Probably never larger than 10 to 15 percent of the total population, Fort Smith's African American population was significantly bigger as a percentage than that in other western Arkansas towns and cities. Although more scholarly research needs to be done to confirm it, racial violence in the early twentieth century may have driven African American communities in those areas to seek the relative refuge of Fort Smith. While hardly free of the color line or even racial violence, the city may have been seen as comparatively tranquil and safe.

Some examples of racial violence then include incidents in Bonanza, Mulberry and a rural part of Crawford County called Catcher. An August 24, 1903 edition of the *Fort Smith News Record* reports, "Mulberry is one town in Crawford County that will not permit negroes to live within its limits, and this will probably precipitate serious trouble there if the negro laborers on the Iron Mountain construction train are employed on that part of the road, or if their boarding cars are set out on any of the sidings there." The newspaper reports a failed attempt to dynamite one of the cars. If it had succeeded, many of the workers would have been killed. Shots also were fired at one of the cars.

In Bonanza a year later, white on black violence erupted, resulting in an exchange of gunfire outside the Clinton Saloon. Mining companies, which owned the coal mines in south Sebastian County, had begun bringing in more African American laborers following an 1899 strike. About two hundred citizens of Bonanza met in April 1904 to petition one of the companies to remove about forty African Americans from the town. The mine company pledged to protect the men, but once violence erupted, the forty miners and their families fled.

On December 28, 1923, the assault and murder of a white woman in the Catcher community ignited racial violence that resulted in the murder

The Fort Smith Light and Traction Company developed Electric Park, located where Kay Rodgers Park is today, to draw riders on its trolley farther out on its northern line. However, blacks were not welcome there at regular times. The company did host some special days for black visitors separately to use the park. A sign on a pole to the right of the entrance seen here reads: "This Park for White People Only." *Courtesy of Joe Wasson.*

of an innocent African American man and the expulsion of forty African American families, the *Encyclopedia of Arkansas* states.

Because of a state law passed in 1903, the Fort Smith Light and Traction Company was forced to segregate its trolley cars. According to the *News Record* at the time the bill passed, a company spokesman said it already had partitions in the cars to separate smokers and non-smokers. The company likely would ban smoking but make the smoking sections into seating for African American riders. "We have had no complaint over the mixing of the races," he said, mixing tolerance with mild condescension. "We have a well-behaved class of colored people here."

Fort Smith Light and Traction also operated Electric Park, an amusement park and meeting facility at the north end of the city. It was open to whites only but did allow African Americans to use it on a limited number of select days each year.

The organizers of a September 1903 "Colored Fair," however, did allow whites to attend their festivities, the *Fort Smith News Record* reported. Several white city officials even attended a coronation ceremony for the fair queen. Musicians and singers performed, and Isaac Fisher, a Tuskegee Institute graduate and principal of Pine Bluff School, delivered a lecture on race relations. The fair also included the elements typical of other such events at that time, like agricultural exhibits and contests.

With the coming of motor vehicles and, eventually, cab service, the city continued to segregate transportation. Although the number of riders in a single cab car would seem not to warrant segregation, since usually there was only up to three riders who wanted to ride together, the Dixie Cab Co. was the only taxi cab service in Fort Smith that served blacks during the days of Jim Crow. City directories don't record the business as operating in the 1950s, but Dixie does show up in a 1961 volume and as late as 1970. None of the city directories identify Dixie—or any of the other cab services, for that matter—as exclusively serving either race. A 1956 Yellow Pages telephone book does have the following entry: "Taxicabs—Colored, Dixie Cab Co., 814 North A, Sunset 3-1444." Several local people still remember the distinctive orange lights on the Dixie Cab cars, and a Dixie Cab orange cab light still decorates the wall of a downtown eatery.

Some other local segregation practices are recorded in the 1949 edition of *The Negro Motorist Green Book—1949 Edition*. It lists things like hotels, barbershops, service stations and a wide variety of other businesses that blacks could use while traveling. The guide's introduction states, "It has been our idea to give the Negro traveler information that will keep him from running into difficulties, embarrassments and to make his trips more enjoyable." Of course, the unspoken subtext is that if it is not in the *Green Book*, then a business may be likely to deny you service if you were black. In the Fort Smith entry, it only lists two lodging places for blacks: the Ullery Inn at 719 North Ninth Street and the E.O. Trent Tourist Home at 1301 North Ninth. No cab companies are listed, but they aren't anywhere else in the book either. Because the *Green Book* was designed for automobile travelers especially, that sort of listing may have seemed unnecessary to the publication's editors.

Most theaters maintained separate balcony seating for blacks, often the hottest part of an auditorium in the warm-weather months before the advent of air conditioning systems. The Malco Theatre on Garrison Avenue, originally built as and known as the New Theatre, had two balconies, reserving the uppermost for black patrons. Some local white theater owners attempted in the late 1940s to open a theater on Midland Boulevard called the Pix for an exclusively black audience. However, its patronage wasn't strong enough to sustain it, so they renamed it the Rex and segregated the seating there, too. African American theatergoers at the Rex also had to sit in balcony seating. They bought tickets at a separate sales window at the side of the building and walked up a stairway from there to the balcony. An usher would run orders for popcorn and soda to and from the audience there.

With the end of Jim Crow laws and the coming of integration in the 1950s and 1960s, these segregation practices came to an end in Fort Smith, as they did in other American cities and towns. The color line blurred, and then it disappeared.

Bonneville's Places

Little about General Benjamin Bonneville's life story is hidden or unknown except perhaps for the places in Fort Smith most closely associated with him.

Born in France, Benjamin Bonneville's family fled the political chaos and turmoil of that country and came to settle in New York in 1803 while he was still a boy. They lived with American Revolutionary writer Thomas Paine for much of their time there. Bonneville would go on to graduate from West Point, join the army and explore the American West, blazing parts of the Oregon Trail. He variously was friends with Washington Irving, who wrote and published an account of his explorations, the Marquis de Lafayette and Sam Houston. It could be argued that he was the nineteenth century's equivalent of the now popular Six Degrees of Kevin Bacon game, as he was connected to many of the major American figures from the Revolutionary War through the Civil War and beyond. He was also deeply connected to Fort Smith.

Bonneville was commander of the second Fort Smith more than once in the 1830s and 1840s. After several different commands in the West in New Mexico and Oregon, as well as service in the Mexican War, he retired in 1861 to Fort Smith with his wife and daughter. His retirement was short-lived, as the Civil War resulted in his recall to service in St. Louis. Bonneville lost his wife and only daughter to illness there. After another return to Fort Smith, he took a second wife, Sue Neis, who was almost fifty years his junior. After his death, she would go on to purchase in 1878 a home that now bears his name on North Seventh Street in today's Belle Grove Historic District. The general himself, however, never lived there.

An area east of Waldron Road and between Grand Avenue and Roselawn Cemetery once was called Bonneville Park, although it was really nothing more than raw, wooded land. Local lore has it that General Bonneville once owned all or part of that. A house on what is now North O Street was the residence in which he lived during his last years in Fort Smith. His holdings around the house were about one thousand acres, so it is quite plausible that the wooded Booneville Park area may have belonged to him.

Supposedly, the home was the site of numerous balls and gatherings of young people in those same years. Despite his advancing age, Bonneville reportedly still enjoyed the energy and presence of young people. Whether or not he would have enjoyed a round of golf is an open question.

Bonneville's house was still standing in 1932 when S.W. Creekmore Sr. started work there, building the Rolling Knolls Country Club. It's a name that conjures up images of gently curving hills, grassy fields and lazy picnics. In fact, it's surprising that some developer hasn't plucked the two-word phrase from Fort Smith history and slapped it on a new subdivision in south Fort Smith.

According to a reminiscence of Dusty Helbling, the golf range included between sixty and eighty acres of the original one-thousand-acre Bonneville tract. Bonneville's house became the clubhouse. Alas, neither the house nor the country club nor the golf course is there anymore. Helbling writes that Fred Hinkle came up with the name as part of a naming contest.

The rest of the Bonneville property was developed in a more piecemeal fashion during the twentieth century. Alexander Leigh "Pat" Kelley platted the Eastwood subdivision in 1949. Kelley was the son of Leigh Kelley (as in Leigh Avenue) and the grandson of Harry E. Kelley (as in Harry E. Kelley Park). Seeing as how Clint Eastwood didn't become a star until well after 1949, Kelley likely chose the name because it was in what was then one of the easternmost parts of Fort Smith and it was wooded. A local realtor said he could remember going there to hunt when he was a boy. The land from Waldron east to the Arkansas River was trees all the way, except for a few farmers' fields.

Bonneville's name may not have lived on where he lived, but it did live on. Bonneville Elementary School in Fort Smith honors him, as do several geographic place names in the western United States. Bonneville Salt Flats in Utah is used for high-speed automobile tests. Lake Bonneville also is in Utah, and a town in Washington state also bears his name. There even is a Bonneville Crater on Mars.

Walter Cauthron, an early west Arkansas settler, reportedly intended to name the Logan County town of Booneville for Bonneville, but an error occurred in the recording of the town name and it just stuck.

Places for the Poor and Sick

History often forgets to tell the stories of the poor. After all, they don't leave large financial bequests or big buildings with their names on them. The working poor and indigent frequently live and die in obscurity, buried in unmarked graves that few notice and almost no one visits.

Despite being in a bustling corner of the city on the southwest corner of U.S. 71 and Zero Street near Mill Creek, a large sward of green that surrounds a bank branch remains undeveloped. A handful of gravestones on one section of the green space suggests perhaps a small family plot for whatever farm family cultivated the land there in the 1800s. In fact, hundreds of graves are there on the two or three acres once used by Sebastian County for a paupers' cemetery. Apparently, the gravestones there are the tip of the dead iceberg.

A Fort Smith Public Library database indicates there are at least 319 recorded graves there. The county was burying the indigent, so most of them probably only had small wooden crosses when the graves were placed—crosses that are long gone. In 1986, local genealogist and historian Sue Clark and a friend looked the field over, and only seven gravestones were visible. Elmwood Cemetery—that's its official name—was used as a burial place between 1891 and 1958. It's quite possible that the 319 total is a conservative figure. A "county poor farm" was located across from it on the other side of the creek. Little, if anything, is remembered about it.

Disease made little distinction between rich and poor in 1905 in Fort Smith, though little distinction did it make anywhere or anytime before the advent of modern antibiotics and other advances in medicine. An excellent example of that is a yellow fever epidemic that year. It started in New Orleans. The only halfway effective response that public health authorities had then was to impose quarantines. Radiating out from New Orleans into the South, they ordered quarantines at train stations and river stops; Fort Smith was both. Mayor Henry Kuper ordered Fort Smith police to inspect all trains entering the city.

People leaving the city had to pay the city one dollar for documents certifying that they were not carrying yellow fever, among other restrictions. Citizens started complaining about a month into the quarantine that the fee was too high. Local militia took over train station inspections, and the militia commander announced that free health certificates would be issued to all citizens. During the quarantine, no one was allowed into the city without similar paperwork in hand. A detention center was set up south of Fort

Smith to keep anyone suspected of having the contagion. The quarantine finally ended months later in late October.

Perhaps it was the scare of the yellow fever epidemic that moved Sebastian County to begin planning for a county hospital for the poor and insane in October 1905, just as the quarantine was ending. After two and a half years of planning and construction, the Sebastian County Hospital opened in July 1908. According to the *Southwest American* at the time, its purpose was to serve "the insane and unfortunate poor."

County officials sited it on land just outside the city's limits near what is today the intersection of Grand Avenue and Waldron Road. The new hospital could accommodate one hundred patients, with separate wards for men, women, blacks and whites, and had speaking tubes for communicating between floors. Insane patients were housed on the third floor of the four-story brick building. Windows there were barred. Previously, and with great public criticism, insane patients had been housed in the county jail. At different times on the forty-acre county tract when epidemics again broke out, health officials ordered temporary wood-frame quarantine huts built.

As public health improved over the early decades of the twentieth century, the county campus was converted to other uses. A "county poor farm" or "old folks' home" also was formerly located near the corner of Grand Avenue and Waldron Road. A September 9, 1952 *Southwest American* newspaper story reports that the "county home for the aged" was remodeled. Prior to the project, it was the B. Baer Memorial Tubercular Hospital, and after it was known as the B. Baer County Home.

The home was more than forty years old in 1952, and $20,000 was spent remodeling it. Fort Smith Junior College (today's University of Arkansas at Fort Smith) spent another $20,000 to use part of the home for classrooms. The house that had been used until 1952 as the hospital superintendent's home was to be used henceforth as the school office and library.

The Baer hospital was not the only Fort Smith facility used for the treatment of tuberculosis. Early during the Great Depression, the city of Fort Smith set up two barracks on eighty acres on Wildcat Mountain east of the city limits for the purpose of housing transient workers who passed through the area looking for work. As economic conditions improved and the transient population waned, city officials started looking for other possible uses to which it might be put.

From March 26, 1937, to December 1, 1958, the Wildcat Mountain Sanitarium also provided care for tuberculosis patients. An adjunct facility to the Arkansas Tuberculosis Sanitarium in Booneville, Wildcat had a high

Wildcat Mountain Sanitarium housed patients suffering from tuberculosis at this site in the hills above what is today Carol Ann Cross Park in east Fort Smith. *Courtesy of the Fort Smith Museum of History.*

nurse/patient ratio of almost one to one and treated patients in advanced stages of the disease. It quickly reached its maximum capacity after opening. Radical improvements in the treatment of TB eventually diminished the need for the facility. The main Booneville sanitarium also finally ceased operation in 1973. Methodist Village now occupies the Wildcat site just east of Carol Ann Cross Park.

Getting There

Rail, Roads, River and Air

Trolley Tracks, Animal Tracks

Mule-drawn trolley cars began serving Fort Smith riders in 1883. By the time they ceased operating in 1933 and buses replaced them, the electric trolley system had grown and expanded multiple times over. The Fort Smith Light and Traction Company trolleys had provided transportation to the city's populace for a half century.

Today, the Fort Smith Trolley Museum operates one of the antique electric trolley cars, as well as chronicles the city's trolley history. Because of its efforts, Fort Smith's trolley history is most decidedly not hidden.

There is one little-known corner of that history, though. It concerns two animals: a dog named Queen and a mule named Coaley. In 1912, the *Fort Smith Times Record* ran longer profiles of these two animals than what it would normally publish for a man or woman.

Queen was found by one of the conductors on the E Street line around 1907 in a famished condition and on a cold winter night. He took her home with him, and she soon began riding on streetcars and making friends with the motormen and conductors, for whom she had a special liking. No one knew where she came from or to whom she originally belonged, but she was a smart and amiable dog. According to the *Times Record*, she quickly became and long remained the mascot of the Fort Smith Light and Traction Company. Despite her royal name and high standing in the city, she was a small, mongrel dog. Queen was no more than twenty-five pounds and stood about fifteen inches in height. Her coat was of a dirty yellow color. "Although her guardians may not be able to match her against her fellow members of the canine family in fighting, they will give you good odds that she is the smartest dog in Fort Smith and has more real, hard sense than any high brow French poodle around here," the *Times Record* said.

Queen was able to distinguish between any trolley car in Fort Smith. She knew where she wanted to go and could tell which car would take her there. If a car that she didn't want pulled up at a stop, Queen would stay put and continue to wait until the right one came along. When it did finally arrive, she would bark at it to stop, get on when it did and bark a "thank-you" after boarding.

Reportedly, Queen also had favorite conductors, particularly the older ones, and would wait for them to come along and would "bark joyfully" whenever a favorite she wanted to see turned up. In the summer, she would ride with the drivers in the front platforms, but in winter, she would paw at the doors until she was let into the passenger areas to curl up near the electric heaters. Every other seat had an electric heater underneath, and she would not take an unheated seat. Although to the casual observer Queen may have appeared to be napping, if the conductor blew his whistle, she would leap up and insist on being let out to bark at whatever was blocking the track to move so as to keep the trolley from being late. Conductors would even bend the rules for Queen, stopping a trolley in the middle of the block to pick her up even when she wasn't at a stop.

Despite having favorites, she was friendly with every employee, and every trolley employee felt a personal interest in the dog. At the car barn, Electric Park, the powerhouse and company clubrooms, she was well known and, at each place, had a special corner where she was provided a mat or cushion. Queen was able to recognize her friends in or out of uniform, too. Some motormen even took up a collection to buy her a collar with her name on a silver plate attached to it.

In 1912, Queen lived with Daddy Piercy at his home near Electric Park. (He then had the late run on Fifth Street.) Although she often went home with other motormen or conductors she liked, more often than not she would wait until he came home every night on the Owl car after midnight before retiring. According to Piercy, she was the greatest dog in the world and had more sense than some people he knew.

While not as much of a mascot as Queen, Coaley had almost as much affection and attention heaped on him. By 1912, Coaley had retired from work and been put out to pasture by the Fort Smith Light and Traction

Company on the picnic side of Electric Park, having the entire west track to himself. By 1912, Coaley also was the only living mule that ever had hauled a streetcar.

He was one of the first mules purchased by "Captain McCloud" for the old Fort Smith Car Company soon after it started with mule cars in August 1883. Coaley saw seven or eight years of service in that capacity. McCloud said the mule was young at the time and the best and fastest-working mule. He was so fast that an ordinary mule could not keep the pace set by him, McCloud said. Coaley was coal black in color, stood between fourteen and fifteen hands high and was "very light for a mule that has seen as much service as he has."

McCloud said:

> *After the mule cars were abandoned, this mule was used to trim lights, that is, he was used to pull the wagon around every morning when the man went to trim the arc lights. At that time there were some seventy-five streetlights here in Fort Smith. One day the regular lamp trimmer became ill and no one could be found who knew the route. It was suggested that we give Coaley free rein and see if he could follow the route. This was done and that mule went around to every light in the town, stopping at each one and missing none.*

Dick Brown, a janitor at Light and Traction, said that Coaley was four years old when McCloud bought him. He was used for eight years in mule car service and five years on lamp service until given his pension.

"He was known by his faithfulness and playful antics to every man, woman and child living on the line," the *Times Record* said.

Brown said that when Coaley was in trolley service it was Brown's job to hitch up the mules every morning. For the six years that Brown did that, he said Coaley was never sick and for five years was used every day without a day off.

When the mule cars were abolished, Coaley was sold to the traction company, along with two other mules, but they were soon resold, and only Coaley was retained to trim the lights. He was used for light hauling occasionally after his light trimming days were done and then was put out to pasture, where he enjoyed a life of leisure.

Coaley was long lived for a work mule, and Brown explained why he thought this was: "I know that mule has been well cared for because I tended to him for nigh on 20 years and he was always kept well shod and given good feed. He was the prize mule of all the mules used on the mule car service, and is still a good mule; right now he can do as much as any of the mules you see around here. He is sure some mule and I surely do think a heap of him."

THE FORT IN FLIGHT

It is nearly impossible to research and write about the middle period of Fort Smith history without running into the Kelley family. They had a finger in nearly everything important then, so it's really not too surprising to bump into them again. That Kelley family was amazing. The daughter of Leigh Kelley and the granddaughter of Harry E. Kelley, Betsy Kelley was one of the ninety-nine charter members of the international organization of female pilots known as the Ninety-Nines.

Amelia Earhart, along with Betsy Kelley, signed up on November 2, 1929. Doubtless, Kelley flew in and out of Alexander Field in the Moffett Bottoms. Her father and grandfather also played key roles in early local aviation history. Alexander Field wasn't Fort Smith's first airport, but it was one of the first.

The following is from a letter written by Harry E. Kelley on May 8, 1936, detailing where the different airfields had been:

> *Let's run through them quickly, then I'll fill in some of the blanks. They were:*
>
> - *Crider Place near Electric Park (today's Kay Rodgers Park).*
> - *South of Hardscrabble Country Club (an open field).*
> - *Southtown (75 acres in south Fort Smith north of Waco Street).*
> - *Alexander Field in Moffett.*

The first two to which Harry refers were used before World War I and were on land he owned. Leigh Kelley, his son, bought the land for the Southtown airfield just after World War I. Nearly all of these proved unsatisfactory because of trees, power lines or nearby development.

Harry explains in his letter that Leigh and the chamber of commerce acquired the land in Moffett. Arkansas and Oklahoma legislatures granted permission to Fort Smith to buy, own and operate an airport across the state line, Harry wrote. "It is regrettable that a satisfactory site for this airport is not obtainable in Arkansas," he wrote.

Briefly, South Fort Smith, aka Southtown, also was home in the 1920s to one of the Fort Smith airfields that provided hangar space and a landing strip to early aviators. Too many obstructions, such as tall trees and power lines, worked against its continued use, and it closed in just a few years. *Courtesy of the Fort Smith Museum of History.*

After World War II, Leigh, along with many others, helped secure the land where the Fort Smith Regional Airport is. That's one reason why Leigh Avenue near there has the name it does.

However, neither a Kelley nor any other Fort Smith resident was the first person up in the air here. James "Bud" Mars was. He was the first to fly in Fort Smith and the first in Arkansas. On May 17, 1910, a Curtiss biplane arrived at the train depot in Fort Smith in three boxes and was transported to Electric Park (present-day Kay Rodgers Park), where crowds gathered to observe the mechanics as they put it all together. Once it was assembled, Mars spun the propeller to jumpstart the motor, while four men held the plane down to keep it from breaking away.

According to the *Southwest American* newspaper, Mars tested the aircraft for the first time, and "a few friends, invited guests and newspaper men" were privileged to witness the flight of an airplane in Fort Smith for the first time on May 18, 1910. It wasn't too dramatic at first, as Mars and his biplane "went skimming over the ground but high enough to see daylight between the wheels of the craft and the skyline," according to the *American.*

Both the *American* and the *Fort Smith Times Record* described it as not only a first for the city but a first for Arkansas as well. The first flight occurred not

James C. "Bud" Mars was an aviation pioneer. In May 1910, he piloted the first airplane that flew in Fort Smith and the first to fly in Arkansas when he took off from a field in the north part of Fort Smith. *Courtesy of the Library of Congress.*

at Electric Park, where the flying machine was assembled, but at the nearby Fort Smith Country Club. Mars's public exhibition of the biplane, sponsored by the Fort Smith Light and Traction Company, was held on May 21 at League Park, the baseball field next to Electric Park. May 21 also was the birthdate of the biplane's creator, Glenn H. Curtiss, and the anniversary of Curtiss's first flight. Lynn Bauter, formerly Curtiss's mechanic, was on hand to explain the unfamiliar machine to the public. Mars made two successful flights at an altitude of seventy-five feet.

The *American* said, "The spectacle of witnessing a man flying in the air with the ease of a bird was indeed thrilling to the spectators. Two circular flights were made in a half-mile circuit which gives Mars a world record for making an accurate flight in a circuit of one-half mile, as all previous flights have been made in not less than one mile circuits."

Before he took off, Mars's wife broke a bottle of wine on the engine of the machine, saying, "I christen the Skylark; may she fly long and high." In the next day's exhibition flights, the Skylark improved on its performance, reaching an altitude of more than two hundred feet and a speed of forty miles per hour. Mars's maneuvers took the plane over the park and surrounding fields, as well as the trolley line, in a flight lasting more than ten minutes.

Although the following day's exhibition was canceled, the *Times Record* estimated that a majority of the city's residents had journeyed to the park to observe the first manned flights in Arkansas on May 21 and May 22. It was Fort Smith's, and Arkansas', first air show.

Only a few weeks later, on June 9, 1910, Mars crashed the Skylark in Topeka, Kansas, at another exhibition. He survived the crash, and after being reassembled and repaired, so did the biplane. Early aviator Lincoln Beachey became the first airmail pilot to deliver mail for Fort Smith on November 4, 1911. Flying a Curtiss Pusher, he departed League Park and dropped a bag of mail on the lawn near the Rogers Avenue post office minutes later. It was the second airmail delivery ever in the United States.

Meanwhile, Mars went on to participate in aviation meets and exhibitions throughout the United States and Asia. According to one report, he was the first man to fly an airplane in the Philippines, taking to the air in that island country during a Mardi Gras or Carnivale celebration in 1911. He went there after being forbidden to fly his plane in Hong Kong. He was one of the first eight licensed pilots in the United States and was taught to fly by Curtiss. Mars died on July 25, 1944, in Los Angeles of a heart ailment. He was sixty-eight.

By the time of Mars, Alexander Airport, aka Alexander Field, probably was waning or closed. A copy of the *Airway Bulletin* for Fort Smith dated June 2, 1928, describes some of its features:

- Landing surface—"sandy loam soil."
- Hangar—"one individual plane, 36' x 30', and one 3-plane."

It also lists Leigh Kelley as owner and states that the airport has no lighting. However, "Fort Smith" was written in big letters on the roof of a hangar.

The land for the Fort Smith airport that now serves Fort Smith was acquired after World War II. Based on reliable sources, much of the land was bought then, but Leigh Kelley contributed and acquired some of the land tracts used there for flight training in 1943. It had two runways. That's according to a pilot who trained there at that time. At around the same time, keeping the airport in eastern Oklahoma was discussed. The closer proximity of today's airport location to Fort Chaffee may have made the difference in choosing it, a Kelley descendant said. If Alexander Field had been retained and expanded to allow for a terminal and passenger service, then who knows what effect it might have had on the development of downtown, Moffett and Roland.

SPANNING THE ARKANSAS

For much of its early history, the city of Fort Smith was without a bridge to span the Arkansas River. It wasn't until 1891 that the first bridge, the Gould Railroad Bridge, spanning that waterway was constructed. "The Weaver Papers" make reference to several small, wooden plank bridges that crossed over the Poteau River to allow for wagon and other traffic to the southwest, mainly military travel to points such as Fort Towson early on. Those plank bridges were destroyed during the Civil War.

Ferries once provided connections across the Arkansas. One connected to the western bank at Commercial Wharf in present-day downtown. Another did the same outside the city at the eastern end of Free Ferry Road. According to oral tradition, local cotton merchants and ginners in the 1870s and 1880s subsidized the cost of the ferry to farmers. It made it possible for them to capture some of the westward cotton farmer traffic to Van Buren by offering them a free crossing into Fort Smith. Although it's unclear when the free ferry stopped service, it likely began a decline with the building of the first bridges.

According to a 1962 *Times Record* story, a group of area citizens formed a corporation in the late 1800s to raise money to build a two-hundred-foot bridge from the end of South E across the Poteau River to what was then the Choctaw Nation.

An iron suspension bridge with oak flooring, the Fort Smith–Choctaw span probably opened sometime in the 1880s before the Gould Bridge farther north began carrying rail traffic across the Arkansas River. That was in the spring of 1891.

The Fort Smith–Choctaw was a toll bridge—five cents round trip for foot travelers, five cents for each head of cattle and more for horseback riders and wagons. Farmers transporting produce got a discount. Paper tickets were used at first, and then the bridge operators switched to aluminum tokens.

Former toll collector J.B. Casey said in 1962, "Fort Smith was a pretty tough place in those days," and he witnessed several gunfights at or near the bridge. U.S. deputy marshals sometimes hid around it on stakeouts to catch criminals smuggling liquor into the Indian Territory, a violation of federal law at the time.

In the winter of 1908, temperatures fell so low that the Poteau froze solid enough to allow wagons to cross on the ice, a newspaper story states.

Increasing competition from rail shipping and bridges diminished the profitability of the Fort Smith–Choctaw. A change in the course of the nearby Arkansas River in the 1920s washed out the road at the west end of

The Gould Bridge provided the first link across the Arkansas River between eastern Oklahoma and downtown Fort Smith. Built in 1891, crews demolished it in the 1970s to clear the river navigation channel for barge traffic. *Courtesy of the Fort Smith Museum of History.*

the bridge. No effort was made to repair it, and the bridge ceased operating. Sebastian County, which had purchased the bridge sometime earlier, sold the bridge for scrap iron during World War II. One source put its demise a little later, but in any case, it was gone well before the destruction of three important bridges in the early 1970s.

The Gould Bridge and the Fort Smith–Van Buren Bridge, also called the U.S. 64/71 Bridge, were demolished then to make the navigation channel of the new McClellan–Kerr Arkansas River Navigation System accessible to taller tow and barge traffic and to minimize obstructions. However, both structures spanned the Arkansas River for decades, giving people access to and from north and west Fort Smith.

Dedicated in a huge gala celebration on May 27, 1891, the Jay Gould Railway and Highway Bridge connected Fort Smith and eastern Oklahoma—then the Cherokee Nation—across the Arkansas. Fireworks, speeches and song marked the occasion. A large banquet that night was attended by virtually every elected politician and notable citizen of the region. Gould, however, was absent.

In addition to providing a span crossable by trains, it did the same for wagons, horses and pedestrians. However, those folks not using rail had to

In north Fort Smith, the Fort Smith–Van Buren Bridge also linked the two cities and provided space for pedestrians, trains, wagons and motor vehicles. It was opened in 1912 and destroyed in the early 1970s to clear the river channel. *Courtesy of the Fort Smith Museum of History.*

pay a toll, just like users of the Fort Smith–Choctaw. Tolls were paid at the Fort Smith end of the span.

The Gould Bridge was the longest bridge in the American Southwest at the time. It was 2,380 feet in length, sat atop fourteen concrete and steel piers and contained 3.8 million pounds of iron and steel. Its cost clocked in at $498,000.

Although much shorter in length at 1,760 feet, the Fort Smith–Van Buren Bridge crammed a lot into its width. According to a March 31, 1912 report in the *Fort Smith Times Record*, "The structure provides for double-track electric railway traffic, single-track steam railway traffic, two roadways for vehicular traffic, thus separating the traffic going in opposite directions, and two sidewalks for pedestrians."

How they were able to accommodate so many different types of transportation activity is impressive. First, trolleys could not use the bridge at the same time as steam trains. The rail ties were boarded over so that they were smooth enough to accommodate auto traffic. Sidewalks, slower-moving cars and wagon pathways were outside the trusses.

If about 600 feet in earthwork embankments and abutments making up the approaches to the bridge are counted in, then the bridge totaled 2,360 in length. Eight concrete and steel piers provided the bridge's foundation, and they rested on bedrock about 20 feet below the low-water mark of the river. A middle section of the bridge could be raised or lifted up to accommodate river shipping. The *Times Record* reports that the passage underneath it was 180

Construction of the Albert Pike Free Bridge started in 1919. The bridge was the first one spanning the Arkansas at Fort Smith that was dedicated to serving the needs of motor vehicle and pedestrian travel between the two states. *Courtesy of the Fort Smith Museum of History.*

feet wide and provided a vertical clearance of about 55 feet at high water and 85 feet at low water. Two 113-foot towers stood at each end of the movable section and housed the machinery and counterweights necessary to lift it.

Chains of colored lights festooned the bridge during its opening day celebration on April 2, 1912. Fireworks and rockets exploded in the air above it, "discharging a multitude of vari-colored designs," the newspaper reported. Rain on Sunday, March 31, and Monday, April 1, forced the cancellation of some festivities and compressed the remainder into the one day.

Aviators Charles F. Walsh and Beckwith Havens entertained crowds by flying around the bridge and by executing spiral turns and other aerial acrobatics.

Fort Smith mayor Fagan Bourland was there for the bridge dedication in 1912 and for another about ten years later.

The city opened a third bridge across the Arkansas that also would be the first to accommodate an innovation only slightly older than the airplane—the car. The smooth, rail-less Free Bridge linked the west end of Garrison Avenue to a highway in eastern Oklahoma. People could now drive their cars across a two-lane concrete span. Construction and excitement surrounding the Free Bridge started in 1919. Festivities stretched over two days, May 11 and May 12.

Balustrades, globed light poles and overlook balconies were salient features of the Free Bridge, which also fell to the wrecking ball in the early 1970s. *Courtesy of the Fort Smith Museum of History.*

It being the Prohibition era, Bridge Queen Miss Louise Golden christened the new bridge on May 11 using bottled water from hot springs. On the following day, visiting state and federal political leaders from Arkansas and Oklahoma met in the middle of the span to claim credit along with Bourland. A crowd of automobile owners scrambled to their cars to be the first to drive across it, although it actually had been open to traffic since May 6. At 9:00 p.m. on May 12, the finale of the celebration was the throwing of a switch that turned on the forty-eight lampposts that lined the Free Bridge.

By July 14, 1971, the Fort Smith–Van Buren Bridge would be gone, along with fading memories of the 1912 festivities. An Alaska firm hired to remove it detonated three charges at 9:30 a.m. that day in a controlled explosion to bring down three of its spans. "Thousands of pounds of steel plunged harmlessly into the river," the *Southwest Times Record* reported.

Also in the early 1970s, two other controlled demolitions brought down the Gould Bridge and the Free Bridge. Both were gone to make way for barge traffic and the more modern, four-lane spans used by travelers today.

Rocks and Ruins

Geology and Prehistory of Fort Smith

Under the Fort

With the popularity of recent books and movies like *The Da Vinci Code* and *National Treasure*, popular imagination has become rich with images of catacombs and things buried under churches and beneath busy urban downtowns. Some part of us always is wondering what secrets the surface world conceals. Nevertheless, no good evidence exists of much at all of interest underneath Immaculate Conception Church at North Thirteenth Street and Garrison Avenue.

A wild story has made the rounds for decades about a supposed tunnel under it that led to the Arkansas River. Similar tales surface, circulate, sink and then are recycled again many years later about tunnels in different parts of downtown. Sometimes they concern downtown tunnels once used to hide from Union troops during the Civil War, tunnels used to hide escaped slaves or tunnels used as protection from attack by American Indian tribes. Although one tunnel entrance was uncovered in 2006 during the renovation of a North Second Street building, research and interviews have turned up few others.

Wally Bailey, director of development and construction for the city of Fort Smith, and then Chief Jerry Tomlin of the Fort Smith Fire Department, both said in 2006 that they remember seeing nothing even approaching a tunnel or entrance to one when they inspected buildings from top to bottom downtown after the April 1996 tornado.

Tomlin said before he was chief and before that disaster that he would help with building safety inspections for the department. He admits that curiosity led him to look even closer at some of the older buildings during the inspections. Nothing like that was found.

Calls to an IC deacon and one of the church's historians also were fruitless. They said there are no tunnels, no catacombs, not even a *Da Vinci Code*–like albino assassin. Perhaps that is not so surprising.

First, Fort Smith probably had as many supporters of the Union as secession in the Civil War. After all, the town might not have existed without a federal fort, and many area folks didn't like the idea of fighting and dying for a bunch of planters down in the Delta. Tunnels would seem like an unlikely place for Confederates to hide for very long when Union control of the wide-open spaces of Arkansas countryside was so shaky anyway. Dampness would make them less than ideal for hoarding ammunition and gunpowder.

Large or long tunnels also would seem overkill for hiding escaped slaves. Most slaves escaped and fled in small numbers so as not to draw attention to themselves. So a subterranean alcove or false wall to hide one or two slaves at a time would seem more appropriate.

Finally, Fort Smith was created to keep peace between the Osage and Cherokee, who were fighting each other. Fear can be irrational and lead people to take extreme measures, but tunnels would seem almost superfluous with a large fort and garrison so close at hand. Besides, the nearby tribes were not Plains Indians, and although there were a couple of close calls, they never attacked the fort or town.

The most plausible theory yet was that basements downtown tended to flood during the stormy season. Before the city had adequate storm drainage, property owners downtown constructed some drainage tunnels to keep their basements from flooding. The physical evidence for one tunnel exists.

In the course of fixing the old masonry work in the basement of a Produce Row building, workers in 2006 uncovered the entrance to a tunnel. Attorney Edwin Dooley Jr. had been renovating the old Victorian commercial building at 21 North Second Street.

Although he said it might lead to the Arkansas River, Dooley said he couldn't be sure. "It's a logical guess that it ran down to the river," he said. "A number of people who say all of that area downtown is under laid with tunnels. It was an alternate transportation system for the merchants down there."

So, there's a theory. Here is another.

Before the U.S. Army Corps of Engineers changed the Arkansas River with the McClellan–Kerr Arkansas River Navigation System, and before the Arkansas River changed the riverfront by significantly eroding the bank, a tunnel between a basement and the river might have been convenient to a businessman shipping or receiving goods.

If the bank was higher, rolling a heavy barrel from river level up a gradual slope to a basement might have been much easier than hoisting it onto a wagon and lowering it into a cellar. Such a tunnel at a slope would have the added benefit of draining moisture from the basement into the river.

Maybe there were more in lower downtown. Unfortunately, many of the buildings are gone and their basements probably filled in. *Reflections of Fort Smith*, without any footnotes or bibliographical references, states that a 1937 cave-in near North Sixth Street revealed an underground tunnel with rough log beams.

What is certain and well documented is the digging of a deep and large tunnel in another, entirely different part of Fort Smith. On March 3, 1953, a front-page story in the *Fort Smith Times Record* stated that a 2,800-foot-long tunnel under the Arkansas River had been finished being laid with a pipe to connect it to water coming from another pipe from Lake Fort Smith. The roof of the tunnel was from 85 to 100 feet below the riverbed at different points along its length. It was 12 feet, 4 inches wide and 7 feet high.

According to the story, the mouth of the tunnel was 300 feet from the riverbank on the Van Buren side. A boring machine dug the underground passage at an angle of about twenty degrees until it leveled off at about 100 feet below the Arkansas. After traveling for about 1,400 feet to the Fort Smith side, it met up with a vertical, cement shaft.

A forty-eight-inch-wide pipe was laid down the length of space and then encased in a thick layer of concrete. The reason for the tunnel and pipe project was to better connect Fort Smith's water system to Lake Fort Smith. Pipes across the river were twice washed out. In 1953, Fort Smith's city water was transported across the Arkansas through two twenty-inch pipes on a highway bridge.

Clearly, there were some tunnels in downtown Fort Smith and obviously one under the Arkansas River at the edge of the city, but someone may have to do some true digging to be able to really substantiate the tall tales of other subterranean passages.

THE MYSTERY OF CAVANAUGH MOUND

What was here before we were here is one of those unanswerables, probably forever hidden. Geologists, archaeologists and other experts can pore over the evidence to tell us a story, but it's not the same as one handed down through history.

When it comes to the Fort Smith region, the famous Mound Builders of Spiro, Oklahoma, were here well before Europeans, but they left no written records. From about 900 to 1540, Spiro was a spiritual and cultural center of the Mississippian culture, with a settled population at its peak of more than ten thousand. Not far from Spiro along Cavanaugh Road, they also probably left a mound not surprisingly known as Cavanaugh Mound. Probably no Mound Builder ever called it that, though. More than 27 feet in height, it lies almost hidden and sandwiched between a mobile home park and residential and commercial properties. The mound also is about 150 feet long from north to south.

It wasn't a burial mound, so don't go digging in it. Cavanaugh Mound has been picked at enough. According to a scholarly article by Gregory Vogel in a 2005 issue of the *Caddoan Archeology Journal*, someone dug tunnels into the east and south sides of the mound in the 1890s. This was well before pothunters destroyed mounds at Spiro in the 1930s to extract artifacts for resale, so diggers may have created them for other reasons, such as to create a kind of root cellar for storage. A farm family, the Stopplemans, owned the mound and the land around it in the mid- to late nineteenth century. A Stoppleman family cemetery also was begun in the nineteenth century at the top of the mound. The Stopplemans owned the mound and the land around it at that time. According to a secondhand account, a Stoppleman descendant said the tunnels were used for storing hay and grain.

"No artifacts have been reliably reported as coming from the mound, or even for the general area around the mound," Vogel reports. That absence makes the mound even more of a mystery. The purpose of many of the Spiro Mounds clearly seems to be for ritual burials with artifacts. The Mississippian mound builders also built houses atop mounds, but there is no evidence of either practice happening on or with the Cavanaugh Mound. Nevertheless, it is not a natural formation. People of the Mississippian/Caddoan culture may well have put it there, but they did not settle around it.

Landowner Frank Etter did build nearby, though. In the late 1950s or early 1960s, he set up a large wooden teepee-shaped gift shop in an attempt to make the mound into a tourist attraction. The effort was unsuccessful, lasting only a few short years, and the teepee structure was cleared off years later. A mobile home park now sits to one side of the mound and a church to the other.

Vogel theorizes that Cavanaugh Mound was a viewing platform to provide a line of sight with Spiro Mounds. While the mounds there are not clearly visible today from the Cavanaugh location, much has changed in the hundreds of years since the passing of the settled, pre-Columbian community at Spiro. Obstacles to a clear line of sight today include highway embankments, landscape and topography altered by the changing courses of the Poteau and Arkansas Rivers. The air itself was likely clearer, too. Thomas Nuttall, an explorer and naturalist, visited the area in 1819 and remarks at being able to see for a distance of about thirty-five miles. Much of the land between the two points also may have been free of vegetation during the Mississippian period, making at least two other mound sites visible. Although Vogel states the evidence is not conclusive, "Cavanaugh appears to be a typical platform mound for the region, except for its isolation from other mounds or from an associated residential area."

In his journal article, Vogel makes note of prairie mounds in the flat area near Cavanaugh Mound. Prairie mounds generally are much smaller than Cavanaugh Mound's size and are natural formations. John David McFarland, former chief geologist of the Arkansas Geological Commission, said in a 2006 interview that basically no one knows for sure what formed such mounds.

Two competing theories suggest some possible answers, though, and both date the mounds back to the end of the last glacial period, about ten to fifteen thousand years ago, McFarland said. According to him, the more plausible of the two theories argues that when Arkansas was a desert during that time, some small islands of vegetation existed that worked as dust catchers, accumulating blowing sands and debris. The small mounds formed also continued to perform the same function, to a point.

Eventually, when the environment changed and stabilized, the mounds were in place and stayed. McFarland said that the physical evidence revealed when cutting into some of these mounds supports this theory. Others put forth the theory that at the end of the last glacial period, permafrost below the surface melted and buckled the topsoil, but McFarland has some problems with that idea.

Dennis Peterson, Spiro Mounds Archaeological Center manager and archaeologist, agrees with McFarland. The mounds are not man-made. They are natural. The ancient desert contributed the dirt and topsoil that became the mounds. Wind eroded away topsoil around them. When moisture returned to the environment, water shaped the mounds into the dome shapes we see today. Because much of the topsoil in the flat stretches around the domes is thin and close to the clay, Peterson said the mounds often are the best topsoil around. Grass and vegetation can further stabilize the dome and prevent further erosion.

Distribution of the domes can be pretty random, but Peterson said some areas may have numerous clusters of dome mounds that are about the same height. That's because they all eroded down from the same topsoil line.

Dome shapes can be extremely durable. Without gophers or humans disturbing them, Peterson said the domes may last another twenty to thirty thousand years. So copy this and save it for your great-great-great-great-great-grandchildren. They may wonder about the mounds themselves in AD 10,012.

Town Branch

Town Branch once flowed along Towson Avenue and crossed Garrison Avenue in the 1000 block. It traveled down what is now a parking area between a motel and Cisterna Park and then continued on today's North Tenth Street for several blocks before turning west toward the river.

Near the bend where Town Branch turned into the street's path, the Bull of the Woods mill once stood. It was a gristmill and cotton gin, and its rival, the Red Mill, was on the northwest corner of North Tenth and Garrison.

The Red Mill was associated with another long-since-forgotten site, a deep swimming hole that was popular with children. According to the *Fort Smith Times Record*, the pond had "many uncanny stories attached to it on account of its reported depths."

Town Branch's disappearing act began in 1890. A storm sewer was built by W.A. Doyle down Towson Avenue. Doyle also had the contract to pave Garrison Avenue. Unfortunately, inspectors rejected much of the brick he had bought for the job. The cost of buying more would have made the contract a money loser for Doyle, except that he also had won the contract to build the storm sewer. He used the rejected paving brick, superior to the building brick he otherwise would have used, and made up the loss in savings on the sewer project.

Although it isn't known precisely where Doyle ended the storm sewer, on an 1894 map, Town Branch is shown as having a new point of origin somewhere in the vicinity of North I and North J streets. With the water flow now contained by the brick and incorporated into the early stages of a storm drainage system, property owners were free to bury the stream under dirt and pavement.

Until then, anyone wanting to cross Town Branch had to use one of several bridges that citizens had constructed along it. In a heavy rain, the stream swelled with water runoff from the streets, often causing the bridges to wash out.

At a nearby dance hall one night before 1890, Town Branch flooded so badly that revelers were trapped until dawn. With the sun coming up, the young women were desperate to get home, and the young men were anxious to open up the stores on the avenue where they worked. Finally, it was decided that the men would have to wade across, carrying the women piggyback. The *Times Record* said, "There was a brisk market thereafter for evening clothes."

In a strong rainstorm, the section of North Tenth Street near Garrison Avenue is sometimes slow to drain. Some local residents have attributed the problem to the stream continuing to work its mischief.

Nevertheless, Doyle's brick storm sewer would reduce the severity of flooding there after 1890. By 1912, the remainder of Town Branch past North I Street was incorporated into an even more ambitious drainage project. Its waters diverted into the growing underground infrastructure of the city; its banks became nothing more than a dry ditch. On June 7, 1912, the *Times Record* reported complaints about stagnant pools of water and ponds left behind but said that residents had begun filling in these "mosquito breeding holes" and the waterless gully with "dry garbage." Soon, nearly every trace of Town Branch was gone.

In the last two years, the City of Fort Smith finished an engineering study of the flooding problem in the Town Branch basin and determined that even at its original construction, Doyle's Town Branch drainage did not have enough capacity to draw off all the water from a heavy downpour. Furthermore, the system was roughly at half capacity because of the buildup of sediment and debris inside it. A contractor has since cleared that out, and plans are underway for other drainage improvements.

Famous Fort Smith

Visitors and Natives of Note

Outlaw Guests

Deserved or not, Fort Smith's reputation for attracting outlaws extended into the twentieth century and the Great Depression era. Back in the Judge Isaac Parker days of the late 1800s, federal deputy marshals brought the outlaws here for trial. From time to time, according to some sources, outlaws like Belle Starr came here simply to shop. It's easy to forget that, despite being notorious lawbreakers, they had everyday needs, too, and a need for a place to satisfy them.

That's probably one of the reasons Charles "Pretty Boy" Floyd found life worth living in Fort Smith along with his ex-wife, Ruby, and son, Jack. He was looking for a good place to hide but also a decent city of residence for his family.

The Floyds, aka the Douglases while living in Fort Smith, resided in a house in the 700 block of North Thirty-sixth Street from September 11, 1931, until the spring of 1932. According to an October 1934 *Southwest American* news story, they rented it from Etta Buell through the Jones and Yandell real estate firm, paid their rent early and always paid in cash.

Floyd's wife told everyone her husband was a traveling salesman working out of Kansas City, Missouri. When someone asked about him, she would tell people he was tired from the road and was sleeping. Later, Ruby told Buell her outlaw husband had bought groceries from her many times at the grocery store owned by John and Etta Buell on Midland Boulevard.

A photo published in the *American* shows the three Floyds standing in front of a detached garage on the property, looking very much like any other family of the time. Nevertheless, Dad had a job that was different from most fathers.

Pretty Boy Floyd robbed at least six banks in Oklahoma while living in Fort Smith, stated Michael Wallis in his biography of the outlaw, *Pretty Boy*. Wallis reports that the family wasn't completely reclusive. They even went out one time to see a movie, *Frankenstein*, and young Jack was enrolled in school here.

Floyd generated considerable press coverage with his bank-robbing escapades in the 1930s. Margaret Burris was a young black woman living in the Fort Coffee area of LeFlore County, Oklahoma, when she encountered the bandit. Pretty Boy knocked on the door of her farmhouse one day and asked if he could park his car in a back field of the farm.

After he did that and covered it with some brush, he returned to Margaret's house and asked her if he could pay her to cook him dinner. She agreed and then proceeded to cook him a hearty platter full of country vittles. So satisfied was Pretty Boy that he paid her fifty dollars for it and then came back two weeks later for another dinner. Again, he paid her fifty dollars.

If you were a poor eastern Oklahoma farm woman during the Great Depression, that was a nice windfall for relatively little work. It also explains why Floyd was beloved by some of the rural folk in our region. Apparently, he almost was as much of a Robin Hood as he was a robber.

According to oral tradition in one local family, Floyd also had an encounter with them over food. The family owned and operated a gas station and restaurant in Greenwood in the 1930s. The notorious criminal stopped there one day with some of his running buddies to grab a bite. While they were eating, his great-grandmother picked up the telephone to call her son, her grandson recounted decades later. Pretty Boy got up, went to the counter, leaned over it and stared right at her. After he was assured she was not calling the police, he sat back down and finished his meal. He tipped his hat a few minutes later, exited with his crew and left her a twenty-dollar tip. Pretty Boy was intimidating enough that she never let on that she had recognized him.

Despite such incidents, Floyd and his family must have otherwise done a good job of blending in because they never drew the attention of one of their neighbors who likely would have been very interested to know their true identities. U.S. Deputy Marshal George Yoes lived next door. Other federal lawmen pursued, shot and killed Pretty Boy on October 22, 1934.

Clyde Barrow and Bonnie Parker, aka Bonnie and Clyde, had equally good luck in Fort Smith and equally bad luck outside of it. Bonnie and Clyde holed up for about a week in June 1933 at the Dennis Tourist Court, not a hotel. It was located at what is today about 5100 Midland. Bonnie was recovering from some burns she had suffered in a car crash.

During that week, Clyde and his brother, Buck, robbed a Piggly Wiggly grocery store in Fayetteville and fatally shot an Alma town marshal. Not long after that, the gang hightailed it north.

Bonnie and Clyde were killed less than a year later. The tourist court, later the Dennis Motel, was torn down sometime in the late 1990s. A Pic-N-Tote convenience store occupies the lot where the tourist court and motel were located. The infamous Clyde Barrow might have once stood where customers eye Slim Jims and reach to buy a Mountain Dew.

The Boss

What perhaps remains foremost in popular memory about Fagan Bourland is a question to which no one probably can provide a solid answer at this late a date: was he the behind-the-scenes boss of Fort Smith for much of the first third of the twentieth century, or was he simply a progressive mayor whom the people elected four separate times? He championed progressive policies in regard to infrastructure development, public health and other causes. Bourland also was reputed to have ties to prostitution and other lucrative vice-based businesses that resulted in his recall as mayor. Fort Smith people seemed to have a complex love-hate relationship with the man, loving him most of the time and loathing him at others.

James Fagan Bourland, popularly known simply as Fagan, was the son of a Poteau River ferry operator who later operated a ferry of his own. He took profits from it to start a successful saloon and wholesale grocery businesses. A self-made man of humble origins, he married Julia Bourland in 1880. Together, they had two sons.

Despite Bourland's success in business and his children with Julia, the marriage was not always a happy one. Sometime in 1894, Bourland began an adulterous affair with a woman, Maud Allen, who also was married. It wasn't Maud's husband, George, who caused the most drama about the relationship. It was Julia. She attempted to shoot but missed Maud Allen at the boardinghouse Maud Allen owned. A year later, wearing blackface and disguised as an African American woman, Julia tried again in the open on a city street. Maud was with Fagan when Julia fired three shots. Two missed, but one lodged near Maud's heart. Gravely wounded, Allen managed to recover. She relocated to Missouri but did not stay quiet. It may have been her who began sending obscene letters to Julia Bourland, one of which included crude, hand-drawn cartoons of Julia copulating with a pig. Criminal charges were brought against her for the letters. She pleaded not guilty and was acquitted. Allen remained in Fort Smith and resumed her affair with Fagan. Again, Julia tried to kill Maud. This time she succeeded, surprising her victim in Maud's residence and shooting her in the neck. Julia Bourland was tried in 1897 for murder and acquitted.

Despite the scandal and its outcome, the Bourlands remained married, and ten years later, voters elected him mayor. After taking his first oath of office as mayor in 1907, Bourland urged the city council to pass laws he proposed to clean up the look of the city by regulating junk and salvage businesses, to appoint and employ a city physician to improve sanitary conditions and public health, to build sidewalks and to pave streets. It also was in 1907 that the city council under Bourland passed a law legalizing and regulating prostitution in the Row, a strip of bordellos north of Garrison Avenue and a few blocks long on First and Second Streets. It was one of the duties of the physician to examine the health of the prostitutes there on a monthly basis to make sure they were free of venereal and other diseases. Prostitutes and madams of the Row also were required to purchase licenses and pay monthly fees for the same. Prostitution remained illegal outside the vice district of the Row.

Bourland ran again in 1911 and was elected, again in 1917 and was defeated and again in 1921 and won. The 1921 election was the first one in which he took part when women could vote for him. Maybe some of those same women suffered later from buyer's remorse. The secret ballot makes it impossible to tell whether female voters or just a majority of voters in general changed their minds in 1923, but more than 50 percent voted Bourland out in a recall election.

Bourland fell victim to the Ku Klux Klan. The Klan at the time was near the height of its power locally and nationally. What probably is most remembered about the KKK today is its deep racism and antipathy for African Americans. In the 1920s, it also was decidedly anti-Catholic, anti-immigrant, Protestant and vigilante. KKK leaders put a heavy emphasis on law and order. Whether Bourland's reputation for ties to vice had any basis in fact or not, it caught up with him nevertheless. Opponents and the KKK accused

Shown here sometime in the 1920s, Fagan Bourland served as mayor of Fort Smith in each of the first four decades of the twentieth century. He was defeated, came back, recalled and came back for a term in the early 1930s. According to some, he was the reputed political boss of the city for much of that same time. *Courtesy of the Fort Smith Museum of History.*

him of softness toward prostitutes and bootleggers. Bourland had enjoyed strong support in Catholic and African American communities, too. Twenty-six white-robed Klansmen gathered downtown on May 16, 1923, two days before the election, for a rooftop rally and indoors meeting at the corner of North Ninth Street and Garrison Avenue. Bourland lost by about seventy votes. His successor, who won the office in a special election a few weeks later, was reputed to be the KKK's man.

As he had outlasted and survived so much, Bourland also survived that defeat. The KKK's power began to wane in the mid-1920s as the national organization was wracked by scandal. By 1929, Bourland was ready to make one last bid for office. He ran for mayor and won. This time, he was able to finish out his term. It would be his last. Doubtless, his age and some family tragedies were major factors in his final retirement from office.

Loss of a loved one can cripple the toughest and most stalwart among us. Fagan was no exception.

His mettle was tested severely in 1932 by the deaths of two sons. On February 5, 1932, Cap F. Bourland died of a self-inflicted gunshot wound. He shot himself while "in a period of despondency over what he believed would be a serious illness," the *Fort Smith Times Record* reported. His brother, Morton Bourland, fifty-one, was drowned in Lee Creek on July 14, 1932. According to the *Times Record*, Morton Bourland may have been suffering so much from the July heat that when he dove into the water, the change in temperature caused his muscles to cramp.

Both these deaths relate indirectly to the history of the Bourland home, which once stood at 405 North Sixteenth Street. "F Bourland" is stamped into the sidewalk in front of an apartment house on that street. The apartment house stands on the site of the now long-gone Bourland family home, so the name doubtless has been there for a very long time. Local oral tradition holds that shortly after Mayor Bourland and his wife, Julia, buried their son Morton, the couple drove up to the house. One of them turned to the other and said, "I can't stand to go inside anymore." Fagan and Julia were so overwhelmed with grief by the memories the house brought to mind that they just couldn't bear to live in it again. So Fagan turned the car around, drove them both to the Hotel Main on Garrison and checked in. They lived there for the rest of their lives. Neither of them ever set foot in the house again or even returned to it to retrieve personal items. Everything was just left wherever they last put it. Not only did they avoid the house, but they avoided the street entirely. Julia died on August 2, 1941, and Fagan on September 7, 1952.

Mayor of Fort Smith several separate times in the early decades of the twentieth century, he continues to have a reputation for having been one of the shrewdest and toughest political leaders the city ever saw. Whether anyone ever called him Boss Bourland or not, at the peak of his power and influence in Fort Smith, few probably would have argued against him having the title.

THE SCANDALMONGER

Fort Smith society may not have ever cared very much for the *Southwest American*'s society page editor, Thyra Samter. "Several people wouldn't even talk to me about her," said Richard Winegard in 2010. "Intuitively, I thought a number of people held her in low regard because of stories she had written.

They evidently were quite recognizable (despite being fictionalized)." In 1971, Winegard wrote his doctoral dissertation, "Thyra Samter Winslow: A Critical Assessment," while doing postgraduate work at the University of Arkansas at Fayetteville.

Samter married John S. Winslow in 1912 and continued to write under her married name even after their divorce in the 1920s. Winslow wrote dozens of published short stories fictionalizing rumors and gossip about prominent people and families of Fort Smith.

Copies of a book collection of some of her stories, *My Own, My Native Land*, repeatedly were stolen from the Fort Smith Public Library during Winslow's lifetime. Some have speculated that the thief didn't want anyone in town to read what was in it. An edition of it is now non-circulating at the library but available to readers on request.

She likely was born on March 15, 1886, in Fort Smith, according to the U.S. Census and other public records. After graduating from high school in Fort Smith, Samter attended the University of Missouri for two years before returning to Fort Smith to work at the *Southwest American* in late 1907.

"It must have meant a great deal to her, therefore, to be society editor for the *Southwest American*, for it gave her a means of re-entry into that group from which she had been excluded—at least a kind of re-entry," Winegard writes.

He speculates that anti-Semitism—the Samter family was Jewish—and the business failure of her father, Louis Samter, may have caused her exclusion. Many Fort Smith Jews reportedly shunned the Samters, blaming Louis for the loss of money they had invested with him.

The Samter family, including Thyra, moved to Chicago in 1909. It's in Chicago that her biography becomes less clear. "Winslow has given several conflicting accounts of her actions during these four or five years," writes Winegard.

She may have attended art school and worked as an actress before she landed a job as a feature writer at the *Sunday Chicago Tribune* in 1912. There is at least one *Southwest American* newspaper reference to her acting professionally after she left the paper. As early as 1911, the *Smart Set* magazine accepted for publication a poem she had penned. H.L. Mencken and George Jean Nathan edited the *Smart Set* from 1914 to 1923 and published almost one hundred works of her fiction in the magazine during that time. Winslow published some of them under the pseudonyms Bruce Reid, Seumas Le Chat, Laura Kent Mason, Betting Calvert and others, states Winegard.

When one of her writings was included in *The Best Short Stories of 1918*, the *American* published a brief feature about it headlined "Former Fort Smith

Reporter, *Southwest American* Graduate, Honored by Literary Critics." Her first collection of short stories, *Picture Frames*, was published in 1923 with the encouragement of Nathan. *Show Business*, her only full-length novel, was published in 1925.

Despite her success as a fiction writer, Winslow didn't abandon journalism. She wrote feature articles for national magazines such as *Redbook*, *Cosmopolitan*, *Liberty* and *Woman's Home Companion*, Winegard states. The *New Yorker* also began publishing her short fiction. Some of the *New Yorker* pieces, as well as fiction originally published in other magazines, went into the *My Own, My Native Land* collection that so alienated many Fort Smith residents.

"The book was not well-received by the townspeople of Fort Smith; many of them or their ancestors were included in the stories, and some of these stories were not complimentary," writes Winegard. "These townspeople would have preferred that the stories remain forgotten."

Starting in 1935, Winslow spent at least two years in Hollywood writing screenplays and story treatments for Columbia Pictures. At least one—*She Married Her Boss*—was produced in 1935, starring Claudette Colbert and Melvyn Douglas. Perhaps coincidentally, Katharine Alexander, a Fort Smith native and successful stage and screen actress, also appeared in the film in a supporting role.

From the late 1930s until 1950, Winslow's "life and career, like the sound of a warped phonograph record, surges only sporadically," writes Winegard.

She began writing on dieting and weight control, including the books *The Winslow Weight-Watcher* and *Think Yourself Thin*. In 1954, the last collection of her short stories—*The Sex Without Sentiment*—was published. Sometime in the late 1940s, a young female reporter for the *Times Record* interviewed Samter and remembers her as smart, stylish and still attractive.

Winegard states that her prolific production as a writer began to decline at about that time. Winslow made her last trip to Fort Smith in 1960. Shortly after the visit, she fell ill and never fully recovered. She died on December 1, 1961, and was buried in Westchester County, New York.

"Thyra Samter Winslow was more, however, than the relation of chronological facts would suggest," writes Winegard. "She was restless, witty, independent, cruel, shrewd, kind, utterly mendacious, sometimes completely dishonorable, and yet she is remembered most for her charm."

The Marshal

Valentine Dell's tenure from 1880 to 1882 as the United States marshal in federal Judge Isaac C. Parker's court in the Western District of Arkansas was marked by resistance from other court officials, political division and charges and counter-charges of corruption. It is a story that raises more questions than it gives answers. It also is one largely lost to time and perhaps overshadowed by some of the mythology surrounding Parker's court.

Dell was born in Baden, Germany, in 1829. He immigrated to the United States in the late 1840s as a young man. Before settling for the rest of his life in Fort Smith in 1859, Dell lived in Chicago, New Orleans and Kansas. Coming from a long line of educators in Germany, he set up "a school of instruction in the higher branches of education," the *Fort Smith Elevator* reported in 1885.

Dell held many offices besides marshal, including state senator, U.S. postmaster and school board member. What he probably is best remembered for, though, is his career as a newspaper publisher. In 1863, in the middle of the Civil War in the South, Dell founded the *Fort Smith New Era*. Union forces in September 1863 had recaptured north Arkansas, including Fort Smith. The *New Era* was unreservedly Unionist and Republican in its sentiments. Editorially, it could be confrontational in its style, and Dell never shrank from taking an unpopular position. After the war, he would even taunt Confederates and Lost Causers by trumpeting the *New Era* as the "Oldest Republican Newspaper in the Now Defunct Confederacy."

Less than a year before the end of the outgoing administration of President Rutherford B. Hayes, the Senate confirmed Dell's appointment as marshal for the Western District of Arkansas. He replaced D.P. Upham in that post in June 1880. Even before a month had passed into his term of service, money troubles arose. In a June 19, 1880 letter to U.S. attorney general Charles Devens, Judge Parker stated that Dell was insolvent and, because of his financial status, should be required to post a $3,000 surety bond instead of the usual $2,000 in order to assume the marshal's office. Later, in a March 23, 1882 edition of the *New Era*, Dell would write, "When appointed and confirmed a most diabolical opposition rushed to the front to prevent the President to issue our commission. Our fellow citizens, who have known us for nearly a quarter of a century will be amazed, when they learn the full particulars. There was scarcely a species of infamy that was not attached to our name." Opponents, according to the *New Era*, even tried to convince Hayes that Dell had been a Democrat.

A self-professed Radical Republican, Dell had openly derided other court officials like U.S. commissioner James Brizzolara as less than true Republicans and as opportunist carpetbaggers only interested in personal gain. U.S. attorney William Henry Harrison Clayton was closely allied with Brizzolara. The two men even were law partners for a time. Dell claimed in the *New Era* in March 1882 that when he became marshal he was "determined to…drop all resentments."

As marshal, Dell claimed to have restored the office—which had become associated with "arbitrary arrest," cruelty and other abuses—to good repute. He improved the bedding and other living conditions of prisoners and even found a way to lower the daily cost of feeding them while also improving the quality of those meals. "No prisoners were robbed, none chained by the neck and inhumanely treated, no severe punishment of any kind ever resorted to and none escaped," Dell stated in 1882. New coats and uniforms for officials of the court and jail were introduced.

Only a few months into his time as marshal, Dell himself fell victim to a crime. Sometime between midnight and 1:00 a.m. on July 1, 1881, the marshal left his office and started his journey home. He was carrying an umbrella in one hand and papers in another as he walked. According to the *New Era*, city of Fort Smith recorder and deputy U.S. collector of internal revenue A.S. Fowler surprised Dell outside the walls of the fort and struck him in the head with a brick. Dell, in an "insensible" state, fell to the ground. Fowler next removed Dell's pistol from his coat and proceeded to pistol whip the marshal with his own gun. Fowler also kicked at him for good measure. Only the presence of some passersby caused him to stop the attack and flee. Once discovered, Dell's rescuers took him to a nearby home and informed his family what had happened. They moved him to his own residence the next day to continue his recovery.

Fowler ostensibly was provoked to attack Dell by a brief report in the June 22, 1881 edition of the *New Era*. It read: "A poor, silly, foolish Bird was snared by a Cruel Fowel, already mated. Poor, little silly Birdie is gone to hide her disgrace, but the Cruel Fowler remains in all honors…Shame, Shame, oh Shame!" Fowler allegedly had "ruined" a sixteen-year-old girl of a prominent family. Her family had sent her, the "Birdie," to St. Louis to escape the gossip. Although the *Fort Smith Elevator* often was at odds with Dell and the *New Era*, it defended Dell in print and went after Fowler, calling him "a devil in human form" and a "fiend incarnate."

The *New Era* asserted in a July 13, 1881 edition that more than Fowler's indignation and ire was behind the attack. "All the surroundings of the case show that there were others engaged in and cognizant of the premeditated attack than the ruffian who struck the blows," it states. City officials refused to prosecute Fowler, deferring to state courts to handle it. It appears that Fowler never received more than a fifty-dollar fine for attacking a federal official.

Although Fowler got off lightly for the attack, several months after it and his recovery, Dell found himself in trouble and out of office. On March 18, 1882, he turned over the job of marshal to his successor, Thomas Boles. "To say that we did it gladly and joyfully would be saying what is not true," Dell wrote in the *New Era*. "But it is true, that we relinquished it without a single pang for so intense, bitter and malicious has been the opposition of the Guiteau Republicans of Arkansas…that it is rather a relief than otherwise to be done with them all." On July 2, 1881, Charles Guiteau shot Republican president James Garfield, who eventually died many weeks later from his wounds.

Dell never explicitly named what the Guiteau Republicans were doing to him, but he might have been referring to criminal charges against him alleging he had embezzled funds and defrauded the federal government of money while serving as marshal. Supposedly, Dell had paid Jailer C.C. Ayers less money to feed prisoners than was required and pocketed the difference. U.S. Attorney Clayton and a grand jury in August 1882 also accused Dell of filing false claims for expenses incurred in transporting convicts to a federal prison in Detroit. Court records in the National Archives are unclear as to how the case finally was adjudicated, but it does not appear the charges ever were made to stick. The *Little Rock Democrat* in August 1882 stated, "If there ever was an honest official in Arkansas, that man was Valentine Dell. Those who know him best will not believe this report." Whatever the outcome, Dell remained a free man and continued to publish the *New Era*.

It's interesting to speculate as to which was the injured party and which was the aggressor. Perhaps something more than the duty of office motivated Clayton to go after Dell, even when he was no longer marshal. What is almost beyond doubt is the supposition that Dell took some of the answers to these questions to his grave. He died on October 10, 1885, after a prolonged illness.

THE RISE AND FALL OF JOHN HESKITT WRIGHT

John Heskitt Wright did not even serve a full year as Fort Smith mayor in 1917 before being booted out of office by a Sebastian County Circuit Court judge. Nevertheless, his tenure was an eventful and controversial one. *Courtesy of the Fort Smith Museum of History.*

As president of a small railroad company, the business suit–wearing John Heskitt Wright hardly presented the picture of a bomb-throwing radical or even a crusading reformer, but in 1917, he decided to run for mayor of Fort Smith and would become the candidate of labor unions and reformers. The *Southwest American* urged Fort Smith's citizenry to vote for him, along with other candidates for city commissioner, for that reason and to vote for the paper's endorsed slate of candidates to make a "clean sweep" of city government. To win, Wright would have to beat the formidable former mayor, Fagan Bourland, and a third candidate, John W. Howell, who had little support. Wright would win, but he also would be convicted of crimes and evicted from office before the year was out.

The rivalry and contrasting editorial positions of the city's two daily newspapers—the *American* and the *Fort Smith Times Record*—probably illustrate the political conflict and divisions surrounding the 1917 mayoral election better than almost anything else. In any case, they present the most complete historical record of the contest. The

Times Record endorsed Bourland, who had served as mayor several years earlier and whom the newspaper described as experienced and progressive, a man who had gotten things done and still had the drive to continue that work. The *American* called Bourland the candidate of "special interest," and particularly the interest of the Fort Smith Light and Traction Company.

Before the State of Arkansas began regulating such companies in the 1930s, utilities in the state largely were unencumbered by official rules. The Light and Traction Company was the privately owned utility that provided electricity to the city, as well as ran the trolley service. Wright, in an advertisement in the *American*, stated that he was in favor of a "law to force a fair lighting rate for the city." He called a controversy over whether Wright had paid his poll tax in time to be a candidate for mayor, an attempt "to divert the minds of the people from the main issues by resorting to old-time political trickery." In a front-page editorial, the *American* stated, "The past four years of city administration and the past dozen years of electric light and gas extortion ought to be clear in the minds of the taxpayer and the consumer. The ballot route is THE ONLY ROUTE by which the people of any city finally find their way out from under the thumb of ring rule and selfish privileged interests."

The *Times Record* continued to vigorously defend Bourland, and it went on the attack against Wright and the *American*, calling Wright a "weak tool" of the newspaper and a competing group of special interests. The *American* shot back that the Traction Company, "the Kelley interests and the invisible government" were "convinced that defeat stares them in the face." On April 3, 1917, voters went to the polls and made the prospective defeat actual. They gave the *American* the "clean sweep" it had called for, electing Wright by ninety-seven votes over Bourland, along with two new city commissioners.

Wright's mayoralty would not end the controversy. The city commission passed a law making it a misdemeanor for a "person of ill repute to be within the corporate limits of the city," the *American* reports. City police and Mayor Wright used the new ordinance to crack down on prostitution in the Row, the vice district in which prostitution had been legal since 1907. On August 10, the police ordered the bordellos in the Row to close. Prosecutions were brought against some of the keepers of the houses, using evidence gathered before August 10. Because prostitution had been legal there until then, Circuit Court Judge Paul Little ruled that evidence could not be used, essentially voiding the cases. Also, the state Supreme Court had ruled in another case that the city had no authority to ban a "person of ill repute" from living in the city.

Fagan Bourland, rightly or wrongly, was rumored to have a business interest in the houses of the Row or at least to be strongly allied with those who did. Wright's Row reforms ultimately would come to nothing. If true, then it would have been another source of continued friction between the new Wright administration and his supporters and Bourland and his backers.

On September 14, Wright showed his progressive colors and led off a roster of speakers in the main hall of the Labor Temple. They were there to celebrate the recent formation of a union of telephone operators working for Southwestern Bell. The mayor congratulated "the telephone operators for identifying themselves with the labor movement," the *American* reported. Days later, Southwestern Bell fired two of the telephone operators who had been strong supporters of unionization. When their coworkers protested and demanded the company reinstate them, Southwestern Bell refused and denied the legitimacy of the union itself.

The telephone operators voted to walk out, interrupting phone service throughout the city. By 1917, telephones firmly were established in American culture and lifestyle. People had become dependent on them for nearly every kind of communication. Everyone immediately felt the impact of the strike, and Wright got involved. When the telephone company brought nonunion replacement workers in to staff its switchboards, on September 20, the striking operators, along with men from allied unions, picketed and thronged outside Southwestern Bell's offices and operations at North A and North Ninth Streets. They also surrounded the Goldman Hotel, where the company had armed guards protecting the replacement workers. Things promised to get ugly.

To keep public order, Wright, Police Chief Fernandez and the Sebastian County sheriff were on the scene with other law enforcement officers. What happened next is disputed. Some group in the alley behind the Bell offices broke a gas main leading into the building. By some accounts, it was a group of boys interested in all the excitement surrounding the strike who had gotten bored and dug up the line. Others said it was angry strikers or union folks who did it. Wright said he shooed off some boys who had been digging in the alley. That might have been his undoing.

The *Times Record* and others asserted that Wright should not have "shooed" anyone away. Instead, he and Fernandez should have arrested whoever it was. Both men had failed to do their legal duty, their enemies said. By early October, the Sebastian County prosecutor had indicted both of them for nonfeasance. A bribery charge against Wright was thrown in for good measure. In the bribery case, Wright as a candidate for mayor had made a pre-election promise of employment. He supposedly offered to make John Vaughn the city attorney.

By mid-October, Wright had been convicted of bribery and evicted from office by the judge. A few days later, a jury also convicted him in circuit court of nonfeasance. On November 13, 1917, a mayoral election was held to select a replacement for Wright. Oddly, authorities allowed Wright to put his name on the ballot, but he was defeated by Arch Munro. All of this was unfolding against the dramatic backdrop of the United States' entry into World War I and the Bolshevik revolution in Russia, a revolution professed to be on behalf of workers.

Telephone operators continued to strike this entire time. The telephone company continued to refuse to recognize the union or reinstate the two women it had fired. To ensure public safety, dozens of emergency telephones were set up around the city where people could call in fires or report crimes. Mayor Munro

Arch Munro defeated Wright in a special mayoral election in November 1917 that took place in the middle of a telephone operators' strike in Fort Smith that virtually brought telephone communication to a halt for more than three months. *Courtesy of the Fort Smith Museum of History.*

sent a delegation of businessmen to Southwestern Bell to try to get company officials to compromise some and end the strike, which was having a negative effect on business. Again, even when talking to the business community, Southwestern Bell refused.

At the end of the first week of December 1917, frustrated on almost every level, the city's unions called a general strike in solidarity with the telephone operators. Even trolley service shut down. Businesses closed temporarily. Christmas shopping screeched to a halt. Federal labor mediators finally stepped in, as the general strike looked likely to continue. It worked. The other unions were satisfied with assurances from the mediators that the demands of the operators would not be ignored. With the exception of the operators themselves, union workers returned to their jobs. Just after Christmas, the telephone company relented and agreed to reinstate the two women. Operators returned to their switchboards, and the federal mediators promised to continue to press Southwestern Bell to meet at least some of their wage demands.

John Heskitt Wright would not return to elected public office, but he eventually would find employment in the federal government, working until a year before his death at eighty-one.

PRESIDENTIAL PRESENCE

If all the presidents who ever visited Fort Smith before, during or after their presidencies were gathered together, then they could play a baseball game on a Field of Dreams in the city. At least nine spent varying amounts of time in Fort Smith:

- Zachary Taylor—before
- Teddy Roosevelt—after
- Harry S. Truman—during
- John F. Kennedy—during
- Richard Nixon—during
- Gerald Ford—during
- George H.W. Bush—before
- Bill Clinton—before
- George W. Bush—during

Taylor actually was a resident here and was stationed in Fort Smith from 1846 to 1848 but didn't like the frontier town too much. Some have said Taylor didn't like any place too much and was a bit of a sourpuss. As early

On a campaign trip in 1912, former president Teddy Roosevelt stumped through eastern Oklahoma and western Arkansas in his election bid to return to the White House for a third, non-consecutive term. He made a stop in Fort Smith and spoke to a crowd on Garrison Avenue. Here, Roosevelt is making a whistle-stop speech in Sallisaw. Fort Smith banker Iser Nakdimen stands second from the left. *Courtesy of the Fort Smith Museum of History.*

as 1823, he argued that the army should withdraw its military post here. He saw it as a waste of money. A factor that might have helped push him to that point of view was a rivalry with General Matthew Arbuckle, who preferred Fort Smith to other posts in his command. Taylor also was envious of some of the commands and choice posts his peers in high command had received.

In 1841, he came to Fort Smith as commander of the Western Military District, bringing with him his wife and daughter. The family established a home in officer quarters near the present-day intersection of Lexington and Rogers Avenues. Later, Taylor wrote that his family adjusted to life in the frontier town more quickly than he did. According to University of Arkansas at Fort Smith professor of history Billy Higgins, Taylor spent a total of about 486 days in Fort Smith during his almost three years as commander here.

Other presidents came here for brief appearances to campaign or dedicate something or were passing through. Teddy Roosevelt had served almost all of a first term after succeeding to the presidency following the assassination of President William McKinley and then a second when elected on his own. After four years out of office, he was ready to return, challenging his friend and protégé, President William Howard Taft. One of his whistle-stops was in Fort Smith and another in Sallisaw.

Clinton, of course, was here numerous times as governor.

Pinch-hitting for the presidents and brought up from the minor leagues is Herbert Hoover. According to *Greenwood: 110 Years a County Seat*, Hoover, then a young geology student attending Stanford University, took a job as an assistant to George Branner. Along with Branner in 1892 and 1893, he worked to identify coal veins below the surface of south Sebastian County. He stayed in Greenwood while here.

Other presidents passed through or stopped in the area for a wide variety of reasons. Kennedy and Ford came to speak at dedications. Nixon flew in to attend a football game in Fayetteville. George H.W. Bush, as vice president, visited in 1982 to campaign for state and federal Republican Party candidates for office, and George W. Bush came through while on a speaking tour as president.

STARS ON THE BORDER

In an age before television, there was only one way to show people a city in motion without bringing them to it: film it. Fort Smith's boosters in 1914 and 1915 did that with two films.

In April 1914, *Romance of a Southern Fort* was filmed. The title was chosen in a contest. Advertising of the city was done in the subtitles, according to the *Times Record*. The newspaper doesn't explain what that means. Perhaps locations and facts were given in the subtitles as the fictional storyline played out in the action above on the screen.

In any case, scenes of Fort Smith in 1861 were depicted. A mock battle was staged between the wharf and the Gould Railroad Bridge, using the local military company and high school boys as the soldiers. George Sengel of the Business Men's Club arranged for the shipment of arms and a large quantity of black powder from Little Rock for use in the battle. The river and boats on it were visible in the background. Among the other sites and buildings shown in the movie were the commissary building, W.R. Martin's home on Free Ferry and the warehouse district.

Two reels were shot instead of the planned one reel. At 11:00 a.m. on April 16, 1914, the completed film was shown at the Lyric Theatre to good attendance, and "it was pleasing to all who attended."

In the summer of 1915, the city fell under the lens again with the production of *The High Road to Fortune*, directed by W.P. Wilson. For a second time, a fictional storyline was used to show off Fort Smith and give the facts of its assets. "Miss Raines," a Chicago actress, played the heroine, Euwine Phortune. Hary P. Lyman was the hero, Oliver Thornton, and George Rye was the villain. At Sixth Street and Rogers and Sixth Street and Garrison, Raines did some trick riding for the camera as she was pursued by the villain.

Filming seems to have lasted longer than it did for *Romance* and took in more of the city. Planned as a two-reel movie, it ran to three. Among the locations shown in its course were:

- the homes of Scott Robertson, Ben Cravens and James B. McDonough on Free Ferry Road;
- the Wolf-Pollock store;
- Fort Smith, the fort itself;
- the Best-Clymer sorghum mill and other industrial plants;
- Merchants National Bank;
- First National Bank;
- the Reynolds-Davis buildings;
- the Van Buren peach shipping industry;
- Fort Smith Rim & Bow factory;
- Fort Smith Biscuit Company;
- Union Station;
- Carnegie Library;
- the federal courthouse;
- Speer Hardware;
- R.C. Bollinger Music Company;
- and all Fort Smith churches.

The locations were worked into the storyline by presenting the hero as an inspector. It included "the legend of the love affair between Betty Taylor and Jefferson Davis," which was filmed at the fort site. John B. Williams played General Zachary Taylor, Helen Louise Pyle was Betty and Allen Kennedy appeared as Jefferson Davis. The film premiered at the Joie Theatre on the morning of Monday, August 16, 1915, to a standing-room-only crowd.

The *Southwest American* said at the time, "Both artistically and as a picture story, the play is far above the average run of movie stories, and as an advertisement of Fort Smith, it was all and more than its promoter had promised."

In the course of the production, the director and George Sengel became locked in a dispute. Sengel became upset, according to Wilson, over some scenes that he thought would be included in the finished product. Wilson said that the scenes were discarded and not even filmed. Sengel appeared to be trying to distance himself and the Business Men's Club from *The High Road to Fortune*. *Romance* was shown at a convention in Toronto, Canada, and in several cities in Arkansas and Oklahoma. Where *High Road* was distributed is unknown.

Several Fort Smith natives and residents went on to some acclaim and fame in Hollywood after the arrival of "talking pictures." Katherine Alexander, whose sister married into the Kelley family, worked almost constantly. She achieved high status on Broadway in New York but also had supporting roles in Hollywood films. Rudy Ray Moore grew up in Fort Smith but left in his late teens and eventually wound up in several "Blaxploitation" classics of the 1970s. Lawrence Luckinbill has done extensive work on television as an actor and appeared in film as the brother of Spock in *Star Trek V: The Final Frontier*.

Namesakes

The Origins of Place Names Present and Forgotten

The Kelleys Are All-Over-the-Place Names

Their family name is in several places throughout Fort Smith on streets, parks and neighborhoods. The father, Harry E. Kelley, would be proud. The son, Leigh Kelley, would be mildly embarrassed. Harry Ellsworth Kelley had a more forceful personality and probably a larger ego.

"When asked what kind of government granddad believed in, dad said, 'Well, a dictatorship, Harry E. Kelley Dictators,'" Gordon Kelley said. "He was kidding about how Granddad wanted to run everything." Gordon Kelley was the daughter of Leigh Kelley and the granddaughter of Harry Kelley.

Leigh Kelley's style contrasted sharply with Harry's. "I don't think he went after things as practically as my pop did," Gordon Kelley said. "My dad was a charmer more than Granddad was. He was more quiet and unassuming. I think he was possibly more persuasive than Granddad."

Nevertheless, together and separately, both men did a lot to help Fort Smith grow and develop through the family business, Kelley Realty Co., and as civic leaders.

Harry E. Kelley platted and sold lots for houses on each side of the road that became known as Kelley Highway in north Fort Smith. The son was honored with a street in his name as well, Leigh Avenue. "That's named for my father," Gordon Kelley said. "He spent hours, weeks and months getting a road down through there to make it accessible to what would be an airport. Getting Fort Chaffee here was dependent on having an airport."

Harry E. Kelley on horseback atop Old Dan, circa 1912, poses inside the end of the twelve-foot diameter North P Street storm water outfall pipe in west Fort Smith near the Arkansas River. The pipe was so large that wooden forms were placed in the trench dug for it and concrete was poured into the forms to make it. *Courtesy of the Fort Smith Regional Chamber of Commerce.*

Leigh's Hollow, a residential development sited and built on land purchased from Kelley Realty between Hendricks Boulevard and Old Greenwood Road, also is named for him. The land there once belonged to the Kelley family, and his son Patrick built a home on a nearby hill.

Although Gordon Kelley said the instrument of gift to the city for the park did not require it, the City of Fort Smith decided to name the land along the river for Harry E. Kelley on its own. It has a distinct history and identity separate from River Park immediately to its north. The property line between the two is just to the south of the amphitheater. Because as part of the gift to the city the Kelley family stipulated that no alcoholic drink could be sold in Kelley Park, vendors sell beer for some Kelley Park events just over the line on the southern extreme edge of River Park.

Leigh Kelley took an active role in peppering a neighborhood just off Waldron Road with names from the Kelley family tree. After dividing the land into lots for sale, he named the streets Duncan Road, Gordon Lane, Weeks Lane and Ellsworth Road.

Harry and Leigh did not just sell land and forget it, though. They both worked at developing the infrastructure of Fort Smith—the sewers, streets and water systems. That work may have benefited their real estate investments, but the interest of the two men was not selfish. "I think it was probably quite altruistic, surprisingly," Gordon Kelley said. "It probably was."

She said her grandfather, Harry, was a leader in using improvement districts, which had taxing authority and power of eminent domain, to fund and support public works. A November 30, 1946 obituary published in the *Fort Smith Times Record* credits Harry Kelley with paving seventy-one miles of city streets, helping to lead the movement to conserve the Ozark and Ouachita woodlands as national forests and the construction of water and sewer lines.

While their personalities may have contrasted, Leigh Kelley shared his father's civic-mindedness. He served on the chamber of commerce and the Airport Commission and was instrumental in public efforts to control the flooding of the Arkansas River.

Although some local residents may have forgotten the men behind the names, the work of the two Kelley men still can be tasted in the city's tap water, felt in the hard pavement beneath the wheels of cars and heard in the sounds of arriving and departing airplanes. Their work is part of the city itself, hidden but present.

Sweet Adelaide

William Meade Fishback, the only Fort Smith resident ever to become Arkansas governor, had his house on a big tract of land on the southeast corner of what is today Rogers and Greenwood Avenues. Other residences fill the space now known as the residential neighborhood of the Fishback Addition. In fact, according to one source, Adelaide Lane, just east of the Rogers-Greenwood intersection, roughly follows the path of the driveway up to his home.

Adelaide Miller Fishback was his wife; she died in 1882 in her thirties. The "W.M. Fishback" name at the top of Adelaide Hall on Garrison Avenue relates to the former governor, and the building has a long history. Circa 1871, Fishback built the hall on the avenue and then shortly afterward named it for his wife. During the 1870s, it was the site of all sorts of events and arguably the social center of the city. Political rallies, weddings and celebrations of all kinds found shelter there.

It became a hotel in the early 1880s and also burned circa 1885. Based on an 1870s-era photograph, Adelaide Hall originally had three floors and no windows on its east side. After the fire, Fishback may have removed the third floor. The rounded arches at the top of the second-floor windows appear to have been shortened to become decorative features above the roofline and the spaces now containing the "W.M. Fishback" letters. Presumably, the second-floor interior ceiling also was lowered when these early renovations occurred.

Adelaide Hall probably as it appeared sometime after its original construction in 1871. Although the existing building today has two floors and windows on the east side, it doesn't here. A fire in the mid-1880s seriously damaged it. In its repair, the top floor was taken off and the façade modified. The east windows may have been added at that time, too. The Kannady Block stands to the right. *Courtesy of the Fort Smith Museum of History.*

Some have disputed the authenticity of the photograph, but the presence in the image of a building very much like the Kannady building next door makes it all but certain that it is the real thing. Fire and renovation or not, the hall has survived for many decades. It has been home to hotels, saloons, feed stores, liquor stores, barbers, doctors' offices, locksmiths, butchers, grocers and more.

By 1994, it was largely abandoned and in disrepair. At about that time, developer Richard Griffin bought the building, as well as the Kannady Block next door to the west. He and his construction company set about restoring the exterior and completely renovating the interior. Griffin had the "W.M. Fishback" letters installed.

Varsity Sports Grill moved into Adelaide Hall in 1996 and has done business there ever since. Happily, the second floor has again become the venue for weddings, meetings and even concerts. Sadly, the Kannady building had to be demolished by Griffin. The bricks making up its walls contained too much lime and had begun to disintegrate. Its roof also had

Although the newspaper is silent on how the dilemma was resolved, Wheeler grew to end at Zero Street and provide a home for the first Boys' Club in the city, as well as dozens of manufacturers, including the Fort Smith Wagon Co. and warehouses.

Born in an era of hooves, the avenue has lasted and grown into one of sixteen-wheelers. As Arkansas Highway 255, it makes up part of the truck route through Fort Smith.

Irish Leader Left a Mark on the City, a Name on a Street

Working in Scotland, Ireland and the United States, John Dodson wandered down more than one roadway in his life—maybe even the one with his name on it. The namesake of Dodson Avenue, John Dodson, was one of Fort Smith's oldest citizens when he died of pneumonia on April 12, 1889, in his late seventies. Although sometimes listed as Dodson Street, the name designates the same roadway on maps as early as 1887 and 1894.

Starting as a spinner and weaver, Dodson moved up to become the manager of textile mills in the British Isles. During an economic downturn, he traveled to the United States to look for work, first spending time in the East before landing permanently in Fort Smith as a merchant, with stops in Little Rock and Van Buren in between.

A biographical entry in *Goodspeed's Histories of Sebastian County*, written before his death, describes him as a native of Belfast, Ireland, and the "Irish leader" of Fort Smith before the Civil War. Before the long struggle over slavery led in the early 1860s to the outbreak of that military conflict, race and nationality became an issue in a different way as anti-immigration sentiment peaked with the formation of the Know-Nothing Party. Dodson "found it harder than the war" that would follow.

Although the sources are vague as to exactly how Dodson as Irish leader protected his community, Goodspeed does say that he formed some alliance with the German immigrant community in Fort Smith and that "hardly any injury occurred to person or property."

Despite having felt the threat of ethnic hatred and not owning a slave himself, Dodson sided with the Confederacy in the Civil War. Probably too old at that point to take up arms, he gave $15,000 in support of the South's war effort. In the chaos of that war, he lost nearly everything he had in terms of money and property but was able to earn it back in the peace that followed and in the booming local economy of the 1880s. Two of his sons and a brother died in the war. Dodson married three times, fathering a daughter with his last spouse while in his sixties. Two sons survived him.

Dodson Avenue was an important street as much for what it marked as for where it led travelers. Where exactly the southern boundary of Fort Smith was in the nineteenth century is arguable, but on some maps it laid a few paces south of Dodson. Both an 1894 map and *The Atlas of Sebastian County* for 1887 show it there. An annexation map in the city's engineering department records its southernmost point at South Z Street. The articles of incorporation for the city, dated 1842, give no specific city limits but state that they should be surveyed and fixed if they haven't been already.

That city limit line just south of Dodson Avenue may have marked the end of Fort Smith, but it also designated the beginning of another community, Sulphur Springs Town. A cluster of houses, and doubtless a store or two, stood at the corner of Towson and Dodson Avenues, forming the community. According to "The Weaver Papers," a "sulphur spring" was discovered in the 1840s at what is now the southwest corner of Towson Avenue and South O Street. (South O Street's older name was Spring Street. Another street with that name was in Sulphur Spring as well.)

George King, a property and business owner on South O Street, said in 2003 that he was told by people in the neighborhood that in the 1930s and 1940s, buses used to stop and riders would hop off to fill jugs at the spring and then quickly get back on the bus.

In the late 1840s, when it was discovered, the site of the spring became a camping ground for forty-niners preparing to go west in the gold rush, according to Frank Weaver, a local historian writing in the 1920s. The spring was capped off in the twentieth century, probably sometime after World War II, buried in the soil of the city like John Dodson many decades before.

NEW PART OF CITY HAS AN OLD HISTORY

All traces of the family farm are gone, paved over or buried in the backyards of Fianna Hills, but the family name isn't. The land that is today the fully developed neighborhood in south Fort Smith with modern houses and a country club once belonged to the Stephens family and was farmed by them for one hundred years or more.

Most people don't call the hill topped by the country club by its proper geographic name anymore, but they can still find it on some maps—Brook Stephens Mountain. (The city also has named a pumping station for Brook Stephens, located on Arkansas 45 behind the Rheem plant.)

On a 2002 tour of Fianna Hills, Ben Stephens, then Fort Smith Police Department chaplain, approximated where his great-uncle Brook's house was near the intersection of Fianna Way and Arkansas 253. He still remembers visiting the farmhouse and his father's cousin, Charles, who inherited it from Jackson Brook Stephens. Ben Stephens said the name Brook pops up throughout his family tree. Possibly, the name is a shortened form of the middle name of his great-great-grandfather, Samuel Brooken Stephens.

Samuel Brooken Stephens, the first sheriff of Sebastian County, also has loaned that name to a major street in Fianna Hills, Brooken Hill Drive. Ronnie Udouj of Bradford & Udouj Fianna Realty said in 2002 that his firm named Brooken Hill Drive in honor of the family when it started developing the area. They also named another street, Marion Court, after the wife of Charles Stephens. Udouj honored another woman, his mother, by naming St. Anthony Court after her patron saint.

That was as far as he went in paying homage to his own family, though. "It would be damning to name a street after Udouj," he explained. "How would you like to be looking for the name Udouj and coming into Fort Smith and trying to pronounce the name?"

The Udoujs have been in Fort Smith for more than a century. Ronnie's grandfather settled here in 1898. Even so, he felt good about naming Marion Court and Brooken Hill Drive in tribute to the Stephens family's history in Sebastian County. "We just did it," Udouj said. "They were nice people and friends of the Udouj family."

Ben Stephens's own home in 2002 was just off Brooken Hill. Of course, it was not a farmhouse. His home was just another of the well-kept abodes lining a side street.

When he was a boy, Ben Stephens used to hunt in the woods of the very land where his residence later stood—hunting game, not houses. He said sometimes when he drove through the neighborhood, a memory or fragment of a memory would come back, but for the most part the land had changed so much for him that it was difficult for him to determine where things were. Stephens has since passed away.

Traces of the past and landmarks have vanished just as the name Stephens Mountain has faded from common usage. "When I was growing up, that's all everyone ever referred to it as," Stephens said in 2002, a few years before his death.

Still, with ancestors buried to the east of the mountain in Steep Hill Cemetery and to the west of it in White Bluff Cemetery, and with his own memories of growing up in the Cavanaugh community, Stephens felt a special attachment to south Fort Smith. In 2002, he still could remember the countryside and the farm that became the cityscape and the neighborhood.

TEXAS CORNER AND TOWSON AVENUE HOMES TO RUFFIANS

Knowing where a street is going is simple when it's named for where it ends.

Towson Avenue was surveyed and plotted by Captain Benjamin Bonneville in 1827 to connect Fort Smith with Fort Towson in the Indian Territory (Oklahoma). It began as a military road. Because Fort Towson was on the border of the territory and Texas, the stretch of the road beyond Dodson Avenue became known as Texas Road because travelers used it to reach that state. Dodson Avenue marked the southern limit of the city.

In association with that route, the intersection where Towson meets Garrison Avenue came to be called Texas Corner. With continued use and labor, trees were cleared and the path was smoothed, but the road was still rough enough that it required a team of six to eight mules to draw one load.

As the city grew, shanties and cabins were built along the road and were occupied by what the *Times Record* in 1913 called "undesirable families." The newspaper also reported that at one time there were thirty saloons within nine miles of Fort Smith on the road. In 1958, Louis Lorenz, who moved to Fort Smith in 1904 to work at the Fort Smith Wagon Co., recalled for the *Times Record* how he would avoid walking into town on Towson because it was a "rough" street where gangs congregated. Texas Corner wasn't any better despite being closer to downtown.

"That was the toughest place in town," Lorenz said in 1978. "Talk about a tough place, that was it. After it got so bad, the people finally got tired of it, and they made the City Council do away with it. It was just drunks all the time, that's what it was."

After the wagon factory closed, Lorenz felt comfortable enough with the neighborhood to open a repair shop for wagons at 509 Towson Avenue. His partner was Billy Vaughn. It was a block long and was associated with

Texas Corner, where the Downtown Station post office is today, was a mix of transient rooming houses, dive bars and some legitimate businesses by this time in the late 1940s or early 1950s. *Courtesy of the Fort Smith Regional Chamber of Commerce.*

horse-drawn vehicles. For many years in the nineteenth and into the early twentieth century, Hare's Wagon Yard was across the street at 504 Towson Avenue. Mary Hare ran it and the Traveler's Home at 501 Towson Avenue until her death in 1893. Next to the Traveler's Home, a combined saloon and hotel, was a fenced area where wagons could be parked. If they couldn't find accommodations, travelers would sleep in their wagons and eat at tables that were provided for them in the corral.

Food also could be bought from wagons that roamed Towson. Vendors called "apple knockers" sold fruit, vegetables and meat.

Eventually, electric trolleys supplemented the wagon traffic, running on a line on Towson that reached to where Fresno Street is today. There, the trolley track turned east, ending at Jenny Lind Road. The tracks at the turn just east of Towson were on an incline. Practical jokers liked to grease the tracks at that point so that the wheels of the streetcar would spin, and the car would be unable to proceed. By the 1920s, the bend had become known as "Society Curve" because of a popular dance pavilion there.

During the Depression, Works Progress Administration crews removed the old trolley tracks from the street. City limits gradually extended farther south along the road and took in the curve. More of Texas Road became Towson Avenue. The name still survives though, designating a street that branches off U.S. 271 South and crosses Cavanaugh Road. Towson itself is now part of U.S. 71B and a busy commercial thoroughfare. Most travelers headed to Texas today seem to prefer the bigger state and interstate highways, but for people in Fort Smith with somewhere to go, the avenue continues to be a road that goes somewhere.

Lost Communities

Sometimes it's difficult to know how to describe things from the past. Most of the communities written about in this chapter are not truly lost, but some local memories of them are. Many of them continue to lend their names to streets and apartment complexes. However, a person might drive through a neighborhood of the city and never guess that it once was its own independent or semi-independent community. That separate identity has been lost to annexation, growth and time.

Southtown

Fort Smith formally was founded as a city in its own right in 1842. As it grew, it absorbed unincorporated communities and hamlets that were nearby. As late as 1910, developers made a deliberate effort to start one in an area that is now a mostly residential neighborhood between South Twenty-fourth Street and Interstate 540 to the west and east and between Phoenix Avenue and Zero Streets to the north and south. In 1910, a post office was established on today's South Thirty-first Street. Mail sent from it was postmarked "South Fort Smith," its official name, although it never was incorporated as a city. Unofficially, it was Southtown.

Development of Southtown started well before 1914, but in that year, a big push was made to sell lots. Streets were laid out and named for prominent Fort Smith men. The north–south streets were Falconer Street (today's South Thirty-first), Gardner Street (South Thirtieth), Breckinridge Street (South Twenty-ninth) and Fishback Street. Falconer was a Sebastian County judge, Breckinridge a former U.S. ambassador and Fishback a former governor. A train track bisected the land between North First Street (Waco) and South First Street (Xavier). Later, the southernmost stop on the city area's electric trolley system was in the heart of Southtown on Falconer.

What makes this area especially noteworthy is that unlike some other communities, like Cavanaugh farther south and Mill Creek to its west, Southtown had its own major employers and some economic independence from Fort Smith. Some Southtown men no doubt commuted to jobs in Fort Smith at places like the Harding Glass plant or the city's furniture factories, but many of them lived, worked and played nearer to home. Western Wheelbarrow & Manufacturing Co. and the Arkansas Coffin Co. both had plants on Falconer that employed the men and some women of Southtown. Many also worked at the Athletic Smelting Co., which smelted zinc into spelter bricks in a dirty plant at the corner of what is today Zero Street and Old Greenwood Road just to the east of Southtown.

Often, chemical clouds of emissions from the smelting plant would envelope Southtown. Those clouds reportedly could turn linens and other whites hanging on clotheslines yellow. Horses pastured too close to the smelter were known to go lame, although milk cows were reportedly unaffected. Southtown old-timers today express surprise that they and their elders at the time did not think anything of the chemical fog and its possible health effects.

Another notable Southtown industry was the Best-Clymer Manufacturing Co.'s sorghum syrup plant on the western edge of the community, near South Twenty-fourth Street. It operated seasonally, processing the sorghum. Area farmers agreed to cultivate sorghum for sale to Best-Clymer. The processing facility was huge, with six tall smokestacks, six giant boilers, its own power plant and a tremendous Corliss engine to help power the rest of it. Best-Clymer billed it as "The World's Largest Sorghum Plant."

In addition to workplaces and homes, Southtown had its own South Fort Smith School, which educated children up to the secondary level. Students who wished to go further attended Fort Smith High School in the city. South Fort Smith School existed at least as early as 1924. It probably was independent and then later affiliated with Fort Smith School District in some way before it was incorporated entirely.

Gene Inman, a 1924 alumnus, said he attended Fort Smith Junior High School after finishing at South Fort Smith; this was typical of students

The smokestacks of the Best-Clymer sorghum plant are visible in this circa 1930 view of Southtown. The water tower to the right of the plant is the only structure shown here that still stands today (2011). *Courtesy of Tom Scott.*

who wished to continue on. Works Progress Administration crews during the Great Depression built a new school building for the kids on Falconer. Prior to that, Southtown kids attended Mill Creek School just north of the intersection of Phoenix and Towson Avenues. Phoenix once was called Mill Creek Road.

South Fort Smith, the industrial and residential area between today's Phoenix Avenue and Zero Street, wasn't incorporated into Fort Smith until well after World War II, but the school may have been part of the Fort Smith School District before then. Mike Carter attended South Fort Smith Elementary for all six grades from 1947 to 1953. He said he has fond memories of the place.

One of his probably less fond ones is remembering having to trek "a couple of hundred yards" to the outdoor privies or outhouses that students used in his first years there. While he was attending South Fort Smith, Carter said a restroom addition was constructed so students no longer had to walk through inclement weather to the privies. Games were different. He said there were yo-yo seasons, marble seasons and even a season of tops. Playing marbles was a very big thing.

"The playground equipment would be considered deadly today," Carter said. Wooden swings hung from high scaffolds, and small injuries were taken in stride. "Nobody sued anybody," he said. "You just went on."

Recess was unsupervised, and students only saw the teachers come out during recess if there was a bad fight or weather was exceptionally pretty. Outside of the school, Carter also remembers a semiprofessional baseball team called the South Fort Smith Smokers. The team likely took its name from the zinc smelting operations that employed many of the men in Southtown. Games were played on the northeast corner of South Thirty-first and Zero Streets.

Falconer (South Thirty-first) was the hub of Southtown. It featured the trolley stop, two major employers (the wheelbarrow and coffin factories), the school and some stores that were very important to residents. Thomas Carl Scott owned and operated the Scott Store No. 1, which offered fresh meat, groceries, sundries and just about anything else of immediate daily use. Scott was the unofficial mayor of Southtown.

Wherever working men lived in the twentieth century, beer was soon to follow. Although Southtown did not have numerous bars and saloons like Garrison Avenue in Fort Smith, it did have a few small, quiet places for a sudsy beverage after work and after Prohibition ended. Two beer bars alternately closed and opened in buildings at the corner of Waco and Falconer. Another operated for a time at South Thirty-second and Waco.

Odd tenants wintered in Southtown—the animals of the Parker & Watts Circus, along with their trainers and keepers. From about 1936 to 1941, they used the Western Wheelbarrow warehouse during the winter

A Parker & Watts Circus elephant trainer hangs from the trunk of one of the pachyderms sometime in the 1930s in Southtown. *Courtesy of Tom Scott.*

months when Western's business and production was slower. Elephants, tigers, lions and other exotic creatures made their homes there. Gene Inman recalls a humorous encounter between an elephant and a drugstore employee.

"The elephant trainer rode the elephant up to the drugstore," he said. "He wanted some cigarettes or something. I don't remember now. Anyhow, the lady from the drugstore took some cigarettes out there, and he had the elephant wrap his trunk around her and turn her upside down right in front of him."

Southtown even had its own airport for a brief time. In fact, it was more an airfield with a hangar or two near the corner of today's Zero and South Twenty-fourth.

Mill Creek

When settlers first named Mill Creek, it moved with the slower speed of the early nineteenth century. Mill Creek and its name have a history that dates back before statehood, and it has managed to keep flowing in south Fort Smith before emptying into the Poteau River.

After researching the origin of the creek's name, Elbert L. Costner in the 1960s concluded that it came from the establishment of a gristmill at the mouth of the creek. Costner said that Captain Israel Dodge, Indian agency blacksmith for the western Choctaws, began construction of the mill in 1827. A letter from Choctaw agent William McClellan in 1828 states, "Capt. Dodge has erected a good mill on the Choctaw land at Fort Smith, at his own expense, which will be very useful to those Indians."

Growing up in the Mill Creek community in the 1930s and 1940s, Pete Howard of Uniontown thought the stream took its name from a sorghum mill east of U.S. 71. His mother thought it got its name from another gristmill that also was east of the highway. Despite the confusion as to its origin, the people settling in the area didn't hesitate to adopt Mill Creek as the name for their community, their school and a major street.

Mill Creek community was not just a small group of scattered farms. It was a bustling village of farmers, miners and factory workers. "It boiled with people," Howard said. He remembers German and Polish immigrants, as well as a few Italian coal miners at Mill Creek.

Along with many other community residents, Howard's father and grandfather worked at the smelter where Zero Street and Old Greenwood

Road intersect today. Others worked at the Fort Smith Wagon Factory or the Arkansas Coffin Co., and some simply lived off the land around the creek growing cotton, corn and potatoes and raising livestock.

Howard attended Mill Creek School, which stood on the highway in the vicinity of Phoenix Village Mall. As a boy, Howard and his friends played and swam in Mill Creek. In the summer, parts of the creek were stagnant, and the boys would sometimes suffer from boils on their skin, possibly as a result of the water. Part of the creek skirted an old cemetery, and Howard's grandmother used to tell the boys the boils were from the "corruption of the dead."

The path of the creek has changed since that time. In Howard's day and later, Mill Creek had a tendency to flood badly in a heavy rain. To prevent this, the U.S. Army Corps of Engineers and the city have channeled it and altered its path so it flows straighter and faster. Like the quicker pace of the urban environment now around it, the creek now flows more rapidly. The community that borrowed its name has since been incorporated into the city of Fort Smith. The school closed decades ago, and Mill Creek Road has become Phoenix Avenue. A name that once dotted the land on either side of Mill Creek is now borne only by the stream that first carried it.

RED ROW AND COKE HILL

Fort Smith in the first half of the twentieth century was home to stately Victorian homes, large commercial buildings and shantytowns. One shantytown, Coke Hill, is perhaps the best known in part because it rested on the top of Belle Point, the bluff along the Arkansas River that was home to the first Fort Smith. Less well known but almost as noteworthy was another shantytown also near the river and only a few hundred yards south of Coke Hill. It was called Red Row.

Pinpointing the exact dates of the "founding" and the dissolution of Red Row is difficult. Like many transient communities, it has left behind few official records or traces. The first residents of Red Row likely established themselves near the Gould Bridge sometime in the first decade of the 1900s and probably were gone by mid-century.

"Red Row, formerly known as Smoky Row, is a string of [box houses] and derives its name from all of the houses being painted red," the *Fort Smith Times Record* reported in November 1910. "Most of the population

Looking north toward the Free Bridge in the far distance, Coke Hill (left) truly was on the wrong side of the tracks economically. The shantytown on Belle Point by this time in the 1920s or 1930s had become a haven for the working poor, with its own grocery store and even a church or two. *Courtesy of the Fort Smith Museum of History.*

are negroes at present, practically the whole of the white population being in jail and among them are many industrious families. [Coke Hill and Red Row] are about a half a mile apart, and the low land over which is the Iron Mountain trestle is a barrier between them."

The *Times Record* story goes on to describe the residents of both shantytowns as a collection of pimps, prostitutes, grifters and sharpies. Most of the populations of each were members of what it called the "never work class." Red Row and Coke Hill men at the time preyed on drunks, stealing or conning them of their money or even "rolling" them when an opportunity presented itself.

"Many believe the red light district to be the only section of vice in this city, but that is only a small portion," the *Times Record* stated. "Few of these games are worked in the red light district for that is too well lighted and too frequented. Darkness and solitude are desired by these gentlemen who never work."

A 1911 city directory reveals some very basic information about Red Row. It describes the collection of hovels as extending from South C to South E Street and from South F to South I Street, all being east of the Poteau River. It lists twenty-two households numbered from 15 to 111, with seven of them vacant. Twelve of the residents are recorded as "colored." In all likelihood, the directory entry for Red Row only records a small number of the residents because the geographic description appears to be much larger than the list of residents. It's possible, too, that they were more widely scattered than is thought typical of a shantytown.

Ethel Jones makes an appearance in the 1911 directory as a resident of Red Row. She also makes an appearance in two *Times Record* news stories, along with another Red Row neighbor of hers, Birdie Snow. Both women, according to the newspaper, were the source of considerable criminal court business that year. The two agreed to leave and return to their hometowns—Jones to Van Buren and Snow to Redland. "I'm getting out of Fort Smith," Jones said. "I promised to get out before dark, and I'm on my way to Van Buren."

By December 1911, Jones had popped up again in a short police court story in the same newspaper. She was a witness against Herman Pratt, who was accused of abusing his wife. Although Jones had kept a low profile and out of court until then, the judge ordered her to get out of Fort Smith or risk arrest for violating her parole.

From 1911 to 1913, several deaths occurred near the Iron Mountain trestle that bisected Red Row. Some apparently were accidental. Some may have been murders made to look accidental.

Shortly after midnight on a Sunday morning in November 1911, Calvin Tanner, an engineer with the Western Wheelbarrow factory in South Fort Smith, fell from the railroad bridge to his death. Pedestrians often used that bridge to cross the Poteau River to and from Oklahoma. Tanner and three co-workers were returning from the Oklahoma side to Southtown. Because Tanner was having trouble walking on the railroad ties of the bridge, he stepped to one side, thinking there was a grassy, earthen bank there. In the darkness, he didn't realize he was stepping into the open air.

"He at once disappeared, and we found him lying on the hard ground over 30 feet below," one of the companions said. "He had fallen head first, striking his face. He was alive but unconscious. I stayed with him and the other two boys ran back to town for help." Tanner died shortly after.

"The death of Tanner is the fourth fatal fall from that point in the Iron Mountain trestle within one year, each death occurring within 15 feet of the point where Tanner fell," the *Times Record* reported.

Probably the most prominent death near that point in the bridge—which the newspaper took to variously calling "Dead Man's Trail" and "Dead Man's Gulch"—was the demise of Dr. William J. Pitman, fifty-two, county physician. Early on a Friday morning in December 1912, his body was found underneath the trestle. The right side of his face was bruised, the right collarbone broken and the ribs on his right side crushed.

At around 2:00 a.m., after delivering a patient to St. Edward Infirmary, Pitman said he was going to 2022 Towson Avenue, nowhere near the bridge. Later it also was discovered that only a vacant lot was at the 2022 number. His buggy was found with the front axle broken in front of the Ketcham Iron Works, between Red Row and Coke Hill, and about 150 yards from the trestle. His horse was hitched to a telegraph pole about sixty feet from the tracks. Pitman still had money, a watch and other valuables on his person when his body was found. A coroner's jury ruled the death accidental.

A little more than a month later, police arrested three Red Row men, including the man who had discovered the body. The wife of one of the men claimed that her husband, Willis Finley, had killed Pitman with a trestle bolt rod about two and a half feet in length. Supposedly, the three men lured Pitman to the location with a false emergency call and then waylaid him. Pitman fell. The trio took fright and fled.

Unfortunately, the newspaper does not report what the final outcome was of the case. It appears the men were later freed, and ultimately, no charges were brought against them. On March 8, 1913, the *Times Record* merely refers to Pitman's death as "mysterious." That same story also announces plans by the railroad company to construct a system of culverts near the bridge and to fill in the gap with rocks and dirt at a cost of $15,000.

"The filling in of the ravine will do away with future accidents such as the mysterious death of Dr. Pitman last December and the numerous deaths occurring on or near the trestle," the newspaper stated. "Numerous robberies and lesser crimes have been committed in the vicinity of the trestle. It being near the notorious Red Row settlement." By May, the work was almost complete.

According to the *Times Record*, as many as fifteen people were found dead underneath the bridge over the years, the earliest in 1893, about two years after the railroad span was opened. Doubtless, some of the deaths were genuine accidents, but the newspaper implies, and some people also likely believed, that some of them also were murders made to look like accidents.

Coke Hill is better documented and remembered. Stan Kujawa, in his book *West Fort Smith*, has collected an impressive set of photographs and newspaper clippings detailing much of its history, along with the histories of the forts, Belle Point and the National Historic Site nearby.

Kujawa reviews several disputed theories as to the origin of Coke Hill's name. One is that the community earned the name because some of its members sold and used cocaine from and at the location. Another is that a nearby Coca-Cola bottling plant lent its name to Coke Hill because structures there were built in part from signage and packing materials with the Coca-Cola name on them. Finally, a third theory is that a coke plant was in the vicinity. Coke is a treated form of coal used as part of the chemical process for making steel. Ketcham Iron Works was just to the south of Coke Hill.

Kujawa writes that a review of newspaper archives covering the years 1880 through 1930 shows no reference to cocaine associated with the shantytown. However, more than one *Times Record* story says otherwise. Under a headline that reads "Does Coke Hill Harbor Gang Who Include Murder in Their Long List of Law Violations," the *Times Record* stated in a May 1913 report, "It is a well known fact that a large percent of the residents of that section are addicted to the use of morphine and cocaine, and it is to that fact that the locality owes its name."

Earlier in March of that same year, the *Times Record* bemoans the open use of cocaine on Coke Hill and urges authorities to track it to its source in order to stamp it out under a new federal law outlawing its possession. Perhaps in response to that piece of writing, the local police arrested a man, Allen Ratteree, who was employed by a downtown drugstore and had sold cocaine to a Coke Hill resident. In an apparent dragnet in June 1913, authorities arrested twenty-four Coke Hill residents, who were tried, convicted and sent to state prison for a variety of offenses. If the Coke Hill crime rate dropped any after that, then the decline likely was only temporary.

A year later, the *Times Record* reported, "One of the most fiendish crimes that has been laid to Coke Hill residents took place Wednesday." Henry Jones was struck in the head with a hatchet, and "a portion of his skull was chopped out." Amazingly, Jones lived and even testified in court against his attackers, one of whom was a gambler known for bilking visitors to Coke Hill through crap games he operated. The other attacker, Frank Burtwell, had "long been suspected of being the source of supply for cocaine in the locality, but officers have not been able to get the proof necessary to convict them."

In another criminal case in November 1914 involving an assault and the consumption of liquor and cocaine, Joe Williams was arrested. He said he

An unidentified Coke Hill family stands outside their home with a local official (center) probably in the 1950s, shortly before the final clearance of the land at Belle Point. Some years after the last families left Belle Point, it was incorporated into what became the National Historic Site. *Courtesy of the Fort Smith Public Library.*

had fallen in with three women, one of whom took money from him to go "over on Coke Hill to get some of the drug."

Finally, in April 1915, the newspaper reported on a local effort to clear out Coke Hill to turn it into a public park. It describes the "several acres of land in the tract and scattered about in a more or less helter skelter fashion are shanties occupied by negroes and poor whites, a large majority of whom are slaves to the cocaine habit."

Periodically, local newspapers, grand juries and others called for a crackdown on Coke Hill and a concerted, thorough effort to remove all its residents from the hill. Although when exactly is difficult to pinpoint, sometime in the 1920s or 1930s, Coke Hill became exclusively white. Hundreds of people and their families, mostly the working poor, came to occupy it. By some accounts, two small churches and even a general store opened up there. Many remember the Coke Hill of this period as being a place occupied by poor, hardworking and law-abiding families.

Parker's courthouse became the home to the Fort Smith Federated Welfare Association during the Great Depression, likely providing services to some of the Coke Hill families across the railroad tracks from it. *Courtesy of the Fort Smith Museum of History.*

Nevertheless, local authorities in 1959 successfully moved them out and burned the wooden structures left behind. Within a few years, it was opened to the public as part of the National Historic Site, and it remains today a popular and scenic spot along the Arkansas River.

First, Tallest, Most

Weird and Unique Features of Fort Smith

Hidden Dimensions of the City

To see a thing, to even live in it, is not necessary to know its vital statistics. If someone doesn't weigh himself every day, he may not know his exact weight. Residents drive around a city, live in it and die in it without knowing its precise high points, low points and other seemingly obvious bits of information.

Steve Parke, director of utilities for the city of Fort Smith, in 2010 provided an answer to one of these: what's the lowest point in Fort Smith? The answer is fairly clear—the Arkansas River bank, which is about 392.0 feet above sea level. Being in charge of the city's water and gravity-flow systems makes Parke something of an expert on the shape and contours of Fort Smith. He said Lock and Dam 13 on the river is at about 391.5 feet, and the intersection of Waldron Road and Midland Boulevard is at about 464.0 feet. Downtown also is a little low, he said.

That's not too surprising because Garrison Avenue leads to the river. Before the first bridge was built at the western end of the avenue in 1922, the street appears to have gone all the way to the waterline or pretty close.

At eighty-six feet, Garrison Avenue wins the prize for being the widest street in Fort Smith. Garrison is a unique Fort Smith street. First, it has been there since before the Civil War and was laid out by founder John Rogers. Second, it's very wide for such an old street. What other avenue from the antebellum period could accommodate five traffic lanes, angle parking and all the other demands of a twenty-first-century city?

Garrison Avenue was by far the widest street in the city in the 1880s and remains so today. Even then, it could boast of the wide sidewalks seen here and a broad span that could accommodate multiple lanes of traffic. *Courtesy of the Fort Smith Public Library.*

It's something of a mystery as to why Rogers—or whoever he hired to mark it off—chose to make it so wide. Garrison is so wide that the crosswalks there are timed longer than anywhere else in the city in order to give pedestrians a few more seconds to traverse the thoroughfare. One theory is that multiple-lane, horse-drawn wagon traffic required a wide turning radius. Another is that soldiers from the military Fort Smith needed a wide street on which to parade. A third is that Rogers had seen the wide avenues and boulevards of New Orleans and wanted to duplicate their appearance.

This writer's objection to the first two theories is to ask why Towson Avenue isn't as wide. It's almost as old and was a military road. Wagons and soldiers surely used it from time to time. Also, soldiers typically would have practiced and paraded on a parade ground inside the confines of military Fort Smith, today's Fort Smith National Historic Site. They had plenty of space for such there and wouldn't have to deal with any city traffic.

Officially, Garrison is the responsibility of the Arkansas State Highway and Transportation Department because it also serves as part of Arkansas 22 and is a state road. So it is not the widest street that the city of Fort Smith maintains. Both Massard Road between Phoenix Avenue and Zero Street

By the time of this parade in the 1910s, the width of Garrison Avenue was accommodating trolleys, buggies and a variety of other conveyances. The marchers here are headed west, passing by the intersection of North Tenth and North Eleventh Streets on the left. *Courtesy of the Fort Smith Public Library.*

and Phoenix Avenue between Wheeler Avenue and Old Greenwood Road measure out at sixty feet wide. All those above widths are from curb to curb.

Stan Snodgrass, director of engineering for the city of Fort Smith, said in 2010 that the narrowest street, at eleven feet, is a short stretch of South Thirty-first Street between Carthage and Boston Streets.

Bright Lights and False Witches

Flying saucers, mysterious lights in the night sky and unidentified flying objects of all kinds fascinate even skeptical minds. People's responses to them and stories about them almost are more interesting than the UFOs themselves. An incident in Fort Smith more than forty years ago involving some lights in the sky led to dozens of stories.

Starting at about 9:15 p.m. on August 15, 1966, and into the morning of the next day, reports flooded into city and federal officials about UFOs seen in the sky from Arkoma to the Massard community, now east Fort Smith. According to news reports in the *Southwest American*, an airport official called them "the strangest thing I've ever seen." Witnesses said the lights were red, blue, white and green. An air traffic controller said he believed they were high-intensity strobe lights on a high-altitude jet. Another observer with an Air Force background said they were caused by a tanker plane refueling another aircraft.

Bill Pharis, then a nineteen-year-old reporter with the *American*, said a few years ago that when he went out to cover the sightings he couldn't see anything at all. Crowds of 60, 350 and 600 people gathered downtown and near the city airport to watch the show above. Captain James Ector, an information officer at Little Rock Air Force Base, came to Fort Smith the next day to investigate the lights and examine photographs of them.

By August 18, the Associated Press was reporting statements by Homer Berry, "the self-proclaimed Arkansas rainmaker," that he had caused the lights and inadvertently the hubbub around them. Berry, a retired U.S. Air Force major, said he had scattered chemicals around the state, presumably to make rain. The chemicals sometimes balled up in orange-sized and pumpkin-sized objects that gave off strange lights, he said. News coverage seems to have stopped completely after that explanation.

One eyewitness from 1966 has said Berry's cloud seeding couldn't possibly have been the source of the light. Some accounts say they were fast moving and seemingly self-propelled. If those descriptions were accurate, then it would seem unlikely the lights were the product of floating chemicals emitting light. Whatever the source, it remains unknown. No little green men landed in a flying saucer on Garrison to reveal themselves as the source of the lights either.

The source of light from a glowing house in Arkoma probably is explainable and its origin thoroughly quotidian. The author interviewed a woman who grew up in the house from the early 1960s to the early 1970s. The domicile in question sits high on a ridgeline between where Phoenix Avenue and Zero Street intersect with Stateline Road. Because of its unique position, whiteness and setting, the house is perfectly situated to reflect the city lights of Fort Smith while surrounded in rural darkness. At least that's the consensus opinion.

The woman, who wishes to remain unnamed, said at one time it was brightly lit at night with white mercury lamps, too. Her father put them in. She said the house now is unoccupied and no longer is painted white enough to be as terrifically reflective. No one ever painted it with phosphorescent paint, as some have assumed it was.

Another myth worth busting is that a witch is buried near Cavanaugh and Texas Roads in southwest Fort Smith. Before the Civil War, a woman named Susanna Murris Mickle died and was buried there. Because her grave apparently stands alone, perhaps people started to believe she was excluded from burial in a consecrated graveyard. She must have been an evil, witchy woman for her family not to have laid her to rest in a family plot or large cemetery.

Mickle's story is much more ordinary and much sadder than that. When she died, she was the nineteen-year-old Choctaw wife of Harmon Mickle. Local legend—nothing documented, mind you—is that her widower was so deeply grieved at her death that he burned down the homestead on Texas Road, buried Susanna there and moved away. At some point before or after his departure, he quarried some local granite and supposedly carved her marker himself. No evidence exists that she was anything but a good wife who died too young.

Amelia Martin wrote in 1978, in an edition of the *Journal of the Fort Smith Historical Society*, that the tombstone reads, "Susanna Murris was born June 3, 1832. Married H. Mickle, October 14, 1847. Departed this life on August 16, 1851."

Tall Buildings and High Points

Fort Smith likely will never have buildings to rival the Burj Khalifa in Dubai that stands at more than 2,700 feet. It also won't have hills as tall as the Rockies in 1969's *True Grit* that tried to depict the area as having such. Nevertheless, it does have some great man-made and natural vantage points.

Although the First National Bank Building and the Garrison Building (the old Ward Hotel) downtown first leap to mind when pondering the question of which is the tallest building, they are not. The Tower branch of Arvest Bank is 126 feet tall.

Greg Burrows, one of the owners of the Garrison Building, said that one is 110 feet tall. However, he said, if you factor in the brick extension of the elevator shaft above the roof, then it might equal Arvest in height. A First National Bank official said that bank's building is 110 feet tall. With its elevator shed, it is 118. To some observers, the Garrison Building appears taller. That effect could be a function of the design. The Garrison has more floors than First National; the brickwork and colors are different, too. It does not seem to rest on a higher elevation point.

There are taller man-made structures than the Arvest, First National or Garrison Buildings. Water towers and antennas probably rival or exceed them. The OK Foods feed tower on Wheeler Avenue is taller. Other such nominees include the Donald W. Reynolds Bell Tower on the University of Arkansas at Fort Smith campus and the control tower at the Fort Smith Regional Airport. It's difficult to count all these as proper buildings because of their different uses. The feed mill is industrial, the bell tower is a memorial and the control tower is occupied at its top and bottom but not in the middle.

OK Feeds is 133 feet, according to a caller who works there. The bell tower and the control tower are each about 110 feet tall. Factoring in the height of the base or masonry plaza under and around the bell tower, it could be a little taller.

Without climbing a broadcast antenna or cell tower or flying in an airplane, the highest point in the city would be the top of the water tower at the top of Fianna Hills. The land there is the highest elevation point. It's at about 740 feet above sea level, according to a topographical map.

In descending order, the other high points in the city are:

- Crowe Hill Reservoir at 650 feet
- a hill east of Hardscrabble Country Club at 600 feet
- St. Scholastica Academy at 596 feet
- water tanks at the top of Wildcat Mountain at 550 feet.

It's not too surprising that two of these five high elevation points are the sites for water supplies. Keeping water up high helps keep pressure up with the aid of gravity.

HER FIRST VOTE

At eight o'clock on the morning of November 13, 1917, Dymple B. Johnson became the first southern woman to vote in a public election. She did it in a special Fort Smith mayoral election to replace Mayor John Heskitt Wright.

Mollie Williams, a Peabody School teacher, contested the claim, but according to the *Fort Smith Times Record*, her polling station in the second precinct of the Fourth Ward opened late, a few minutes after 8:00 a.m. Poll books recorded the time of Johnson's vote, as well as the place—the second precinct of the Second Ward.

In February 1917, the Arkansas legislature passed and Governor Charles Brough signed into law a measure allowing women to vote in party

Dymple Johnson was the first female dental assistant in the state of Arkansas. On November 13, 1917, she became the first southern woman to cast a public vote. Johnson did it in a special mayoral primary election on that date. *Courtesy of the Fort Smith Public Library.*

primaries. Technically, Johnson did not cast a general election vote, but practically she did. Arch Munro, the winner of the November 13 contest, was the only name to appear on the general election ballot two weeks later. Statewide primaries in Arkansas in which women could vote were not held until May 1918. Arkansas was the first southern state to allow any voting by women, and Fort Smith was the first Arkansas city to allow women to vote. Johnson was its first female voter.

However, the circumstances that produced the special election are far more complex and interesting than just Dymple's story. The chain of events leading to the 1917 plebiscite was one begun by women. Most of those women involved likely favored being allowed to vote, but their actions in September 1917 had nothing directly to do with women's suffrage.

Early that month, Fort Smith women employed at the Holland-American Fruit Products Co. canning factory signed an agreement to return to work following a strike of several days. They were to receive pay of $1.10 daily. That was considered an improvement over the piece-rate with which they had been paid before. The deal also included a nine-hour workday and overtime for time beyond that. Holland-American also agreed not to fire or punish the workers who had led the women to organize a union.

The same thing could not be said for Southwestern Bell in Fort Smith, which fired two female telephone operators for their efforts to unionize their co-workers. Female telephone operators working in the telephone company's city operations, perhaps inspired by the canning women, organized as a labor union in early September. Mayor Wright, along with the members of several other unions, gathered in the main hall of the city's Labor Temple to congratulate the telephone operators on coming together as a workforce to found the union. It was less than a week later that the firing occurred.

In an act of solidarity, the telephone operators voted during a meeting at the temple to strike. A grievance committee of the Central Trades Council agreed to approach Southwestern Bell management to try to negotiate a settlement that would reinstate the two women. The *Southwest American* reported that the operators were reluctant to strike for fear of disrupting the operations of businesses and other institutions in Fort Smith. C.A. Vedder, Southwestern Bell district manager, refused to talk with members of the grievance committee or recognize the new operators' union. The women at the switchboards walked out. Van Buren operators acted likewise in solidarity.

Tensions between the telephone company and the striking women escalated the next day, when Bell brought in nonunion replacement workers, commonly called scabs. In picketing around the company's main offices at North Ninth and South A Streets, the women were joined by men from other unions. Although the exact circumstances are unclear, a group of people dug up the ground in an alley and destroyed a gas line leading into the building. One account pins the blame for the vandalism on a group of delinquent youths who had come down to watch the commotion at the telephone company. Another finds the strikers guilty.

Nevertheless, Wright and Fort Smith police chief Fernandez were present or perhaps even witnesses to the incident. They also were there along with the county sheriff to ensure that violence did not occur between the strikers and their supporters and the scabs holed up in the Goldman Hotel with armed guards. That night, an exchange of gunfire between local law enforcement officers and the guards almost took place when the latter drew their weapons on the officers inside a stairwell of the hotel. Eventually, the scabs made their way safely to a train station out of the city.

Phone service continued to suffer and virtually cease. Tuesday, October 2 was the tenth day without telephone service in the city.

Meanwhile, a Sebastian County Circuit Court grand jury indicted Wright and Fernandez for nonfeasance of office. It also indicted Wright for bribery in an unrelated case involving a pre-election promise of a job to a supporter.

Strikers in September 1917 picketed and protested at the offices of Southwestern Bell in Fort Smith on a corner of the intersection of South A and North Ninth Streets. Telephone operators recently had organized a union. Operators walked out on strike when the company fired two strongly pro-union employees. *Courtesy of the Fort Smith Museum of History.*

He was convicted and removed from office. In a separate trial, a jury convicted Wright later in October for nonfeasance.

A special election was called for November 13, and inexplicably, Wright was allowed to run again. Arch Munro beat him in the race by about 200 votes. Some of those 200 doubtless came from the 422 women who had paid poll taxes and were eligible to cast ballots. Wright's attorney argued unsuccessfully in a court brief that their votes were ineligible because many of them had not been properly registered.

Munro put together a delegation of businessmen who went to the telephone company to ask it to work out some settlement with the telephone operators' union and restore telephone service. Vedder refused. With both the city's businessmen and labor unions stymied and frustrated by the telephone company's intransigence, a general strike was called in early December that all but completely shut down business in the city for several days.

Federal mediators intervened, and the union workers returned to work. The telephone operators continued to stay out until just after Christmas, when the mediators brokered a meeting between the two sides. Out of

According to the report of a federal commission and the testimony in federal court of striking telephone operators, Southwestern Bell underpaid the operators, forcing them to live with family or work extra jobs because they could not earn a living wage in 1917. *Courtesy of the Fort Smith Museum of History.*

that meeting, Southwestern Bell agreed to reinstate the two women, and the operators returned to work. Demands regarding wages and working conditions were to be settled later by the federal mediator.

OLDEST AND ESTABLISHED

What lasts often is what is remembered best because it still has a presence in our own time. Often, though, we remain unaware of these things and ages because they always have been there, fitting seamlessly into memory and awareness. An example is Marble Hall, the oldest building on Garrison Avenue. Built in 1869 by E.B. Bright, its elegant appearance with simple block construction is free of excess adornment. The oldest building in the city likely is the Commissary Building, circa 1838, dating from the construction of the second fort.

Built in 1869, Marble Hall is the oldest building on Garrison Avenue. It beats Adelaide Hall by about two years, but the Commissary Building at the National Historic Site and the Knobel Brewery on North Third Street are older. *Courtesy of the Fort Smith Regional Chamber of Commerce.*

Pete's Place, opened in 1933 on Rogers Avenue, could be called the oldest restaurant in the city, but it has moved and changed its name to Re-Pete's. It remains a favorite local eatery nevertheless. *Courtesy of the Fort Smith Museum of History.*

Restaurants come and go, often lasting less than a lifetime. It is a tough business, often with thin profit margins and long hours. Not many have been in Fort Smith fifty years or more. Re-Pete's Place on U.S. 71 South is the oldest by at least one measure. The owners of the original Pete's Place on Rogers Avenue opened Re-Pete's in 1985, so it's essentially the same restaurant with a slightly different name and in a different location. Pete's Place was opened by Pete Schmidt in 1933. Although it operated in more than one location on or about Rogers, Pete's stayed within the same general area for many decades.

By a stricter set of criteria—operating in the same location under the same name for its entire lifespan as an eatery, Ed Walker's Drive-In is the oldest. It opened in 1943, just ten years after Pete's Place, at 1500 Towson Avenue. Since it opened, it has continued to operate through ownership changes and to offer curbside beer through changes in law, too.

Walker's is grandfathered in under state law. (That means that although no new licenses have been issued to permit an establishment to deliver beer curbside to customers, Walker's is exempt from any later prohibition against it under the old permit.) Ed Walker's reportedly is the last drive-in restaurant in Arkansas that can legally deliver beer to your car or vehicle. It

Ed Walker's Drive-In at 1500 Towson Avenue opened for business in 1943. It has continued to operate there under the same name but with different owners. Walker's also is reported to be one of only two establishments in the United States that is allowed to deliver curbside beer to a customer's car. That beer still must be consumed on site. *Photo by Mark Mondier.*

could even be one of the last two nationwide if the claims of the restaurant's management are true. Ed Walker's personnel enforce all the other pertinent laws about beer and to whom it can be served and how. A customer can't walk in, order a beer and take it to his car. However, someone can order it from a car or inside and wait for it be delivered to the vehicle. Most people don't park at the drive-in and sit and drink but do have one beer with food and leave. Customers who want to do otherwise go elsewhere sooner rather than later.

Both White Spot No. 1 (1701 Rogers Avenue) and the Red Barn Steakhouse (3716 Newlon Road) are about fifty years old or more. They're listed in a 1961 city directory.

List of Sources

Author's Note: This is a work of popular history, not an academic one. Primary sources, namely newspaper stories and reports, were key to the work. The following is offered to give the reader a fuller picture of what source material was used. In the text, I have tried to be clear about the source from which I have drawn facts and quotes.

American Social Health Association. "Commercialized Prostitution Conditions in Fort Smith, Arkansas and environs (Fort Chaffee)." Unpublished, 1962, 1965, 1966.

Fort Smith Times Record, chiefly from editions published between 1903 and 1916.

Huey, Harry. "Flashbacks." Unpublished memoir, 1970.

Journal of the Fort Smith Historical Society (1977–2011).

Southwest American, chiefly from editions published between 1907 and 1910, 1917.

Steel, Nancy, ed. "Insight 2000," *Southwest Times Record*, 1999.

Vogel, Gregory. "Cavanaugh: A Late Prehistoric Platform Mound in Western Arkansas." *Caddoan Archeology Journal* 14 (2005): 35–63.

Weaver, J.F. "The Weaver Papers." Typescript copy of unpublished "Early History of Fort Smith," chiefly from articles by Weaver that appeared in the *Fort Smith Times Record* and the *Fort Smith Elevator* from 1896 to 1928. University of Arkansas Library Special Collections.

About the Author

Ben Boulden is a Fort Smith native. Except for much of the 1980s, he has lived in the city his entire life.

In 1986, he earned a bachelor's degree in history from the University of Missouri, studied abroad for one year at the University of Manchester in the UK and earned his master's degree in history from the University of Arkansas in 1992. Boulden taught courses in Arkansas history and America in the Gilded Age at what was then Westark College from 1999 to 2002.

He has served as vice-president of the Fort Smith Historical Society, worked on the *Journal of the Fort Smith Historical Society* for several years, was the creator of fortsmithhistory.org and served for four years on the board of the Fort Smith Museum of History, including a year as museum president.

Since 1995, he has worked in a variety of capacities at the *Times Record*, most recently and for the last seven years as a reporter and columnist. Boulden has written the weekly "Inquire Within" column for the *Times Record* for more than seven years, in which forum he has answered probably hundreds of questions regarding local history. He has been married to Jennifer Boulden since 2005.